THE ———————

VIRTUAL PRESENTER'S PLAYBOOK

250+ ideas for rocking your next webinar, webcast, or virtual class

Roger Courville

The Virtual Presenter's Playbook
by Roger Courville © 2015

Print ISBN: 978-0-9965201-0-2
eBook ISBN: 978-0-9965201-1-9

Lead Editor: Jennifer Regner
Cover and Interior Design by: Fusion Creative Works, fusioncw.com

For more information, contact: Roger Courville at +1.503.329.1662, roger@rogercourville.com, @rogercourville, or via carrier pigeon.

Interested in bulk purchases or distributing the eBook en masse? Give a ring.

Published by:

1080 Group, LLC
24111 NE Halsey Street, Suite 200
Troutdale, Oregon, 97060 USA
+1.503.329.1662

First Printing
Printed in the United States of America

This book compliments of

DEDICATION

Scott Driscoll

For faith—without which I'd not have a chance
to do what I'm called to do.

Vince Epperly

For your gift of lifelong friendship manifest.

Mark Corcoran, Sovann Pen, John Willsea,
Justin Foster, Michael Santarcangelo

For being my board.

Tamar, Maia, and Alden Courville

For being the reason to stay focused on love.

CONTENTS

FOREWORD

You might already know that Roger Courville is an author and teacher and old-timer in the web conferencing industry.

Here's what you might not know.

Leading the teams as Sr. Product Line Director, GoToTraining & Talkboard here at Citrix, we see all the work that goes into helping you be successful with instructor led training and teaching: the industry trends, competitive analyses, product roadmaps, content creation, careful planning, budgets, and the thousand other moving parts behind the scenes. We saw the 23-page analysis Roger and his team did when they conducted a 1200-person video conferencing study for us. We see the results of how people grow their reach and opportunities with GoToTraining and GoToWebinar when they attend our free online events (including Roger's). That's an important way Citrix does its business while educating and informing people about rich topics.

But there's more to it than that.

None of us win if you don't win. We don't win unless you are more effective with a Citrix product than with another alternative, or unless you are creating real value for yourself and others and ultimately your customers.

That's what keeps us excited to serve you with great software-as-a-service, but there's still more to it than just the sum of those parts.

It's called "a better life." Maybe you spend one more night with someone you love. Maybe you manage to train a disaster relief team somewhere that you otherwise couldn't reach. Maybe you otherwise feel awesome at the end of the day because something *really* important to you got done while meeting, training, or presenting remotely while staying closer to those important people in your world.

That is the power of what we get to do here at Citrix. It's why we're glad to partner with Roger on getting you this book. Here's to wishing you many successes and real impact with your webinars and virtual classes.

Doug Sillers
Citrix Mobility Apps

INTRODUCTION

"How do you engage an audience that you can't see?"

The question is one I've answered a thousand times. This time, though, I answered it differently.

"You know what the secret is?" I asked.

I paused with one of those pauses so pregnant that everyone leaned forward in their chairs.

"I love them."

The looks on their faces were priceless. And it changed my life. Here's why.

The world is swimming with (drowning in?) information. Even about webinars, webcasts, and virtual classes. And I've had the good fortune of contributing significantly to this body of work and do what I love (innovating and teaching).

Here's the problem. After sixteen years in the industry and a zillion online sessions, any comprehensive book I'd write on the subject would be so long nobody would read it. I know—I started to write "the one," and before I canned that idea it was more than 50,000 words and barely halfway done. And that was just for the instructional stuff before I got to the stories and bloopers and industry trend analyses and vendor comparisons and . . . oh my.

For this book I asked myself, *"What kind of book would I wish I'd had when I had an intermediate level of knowledge already?"*

There are multiples, actually. One type would be a collection of stories, successes and bloopers, and to be sure, I've got more stories than I can count. The other type, however, would be practical and shared in enough detail so that I could really chew on it so as to advance in mastery.

This book is one of the latter—deep enough wisdom to be useful, short enough and formatted to be approachable, and purposefully incomplete.

If you're looking for a beginner's "Seven Easy Steps" tome, this isn't it. If you've got a working familiarity with web conferencing, this will introduce nuggets of wisdom that will help you soar higher and faster.

For those of us who teach, there's another implicit lesson in all of this: there will forever be value in real-time consultation that diagnoses and applies wisdom in hyper-specific situations. You as the knowledge source aren't paid for all you know, and you're not even paid because someone can't go figure it out on their own—you're worth real money because as a trainer, facilitator, subject matter expert, consultant, or swami you help someone save the time and expense doing the investigating and learning by trial and error.

I give you this book, in part because of a generous sponsorship by a longtime client, Citrix (the "GoTo" folks).

I give it to you in part because I groan every time someone tells me they sat through a crappy session (which is a lot of groaning!). It doesn't have to be that way.

And I give it to you in part because loving on you is the right thing to do in the world, and somehow out of that love enough clients bubble up who otherwise realize I just made or saved them more money than I cost kindly exchange a few rupees for my help.

May your audience of learners be blessed because you haven't stopped being a learner yourself.

Peace.
-R

GET THE MOST FROM THIS BOOK

This book is different than many, and there are a number of reasons.

1. I'm assuming you're not brand new to webinars and virtual classes (it'll be useful even if you're brand new, but it's not a "step by step guide").

2. I wanted to accommodate both print and modern learning, and the latter usually means that you consume content over time and go deep in specific areas.

3. I wanted to cover some areas in a depth that no other book on webinars/virtual classes has ever done.

4. I wanted a book to be able to provide a blended learning experience.

To this end, take these things to heart to get the most out of your time investment:

Reference, don't read

If you want to read cover-to-cover, many blessings to you. What I'm guessing you'll find most useful, however, is becoming generally familiar with it so you know where to find stuff later—and then grabbing tips and strategies as you go and grow into them.

Get the extra stuff

I've set up a special URL and password where you can find stuff that either can't go in print (e.g., a webinar recording) or didn't go in print (because I could get it to you in another way). *There is no "opt-in" form here. If you want to be on my mailing list, you can do that separately. Why? There are no strings attached.*

1. Go to www.thevirtualpresenter.com/playbookextras

2. Use this password: alwayslearning (no spaces)

Note, too, that I may add stuff from time to time. Check back.

Join Virtual Presenters and Facilitators, a Facebook group/community of practice

1000+ people will bring a whole new dimension to your learning.

Go to https://www.facebook.com/groups/683685275052439/
(or find the link on the lower right side of www.thevirtualpresenter.com).

Contact me

Seriously. I mean it. Why? Because my first love is helping people, your first call is always free, and there's no way sixteen years of experience could go into a book. And I've never had anyone abuse the intent of the offer (in other words, if it makes sense to work together, real people being real with each other means you know I don't feed the kids with free phone calls).

+1.503.329.1662 or roger@thevirtualpresenter.com

CHAPTER 1

Thinking Strategically

EIGHT WAYS WEB CONFERENCING CREATES VALUE BEYOND SAVING TRAVEL EXPENSES

Most organizations tend to see web conferencing (the technology that enables webinar virtual classes) in one way. You, however, are not "most" anything, and part of your goal should not only be as an expert who presents or facilitates with aplomb, but as a trusted advisor who helps others understand the whole impact of your session or program.

1. Increase attentiveness

There's no such thing as 100% attention. Visual and interactive elements that go beyond a telephone-only conference call add opportunity to move the needle in a positive direction. So much better for getting your message through.

2. Increase visual impact

We know from scientific research that, barring some impairment, vision trumps all other senses. It's a cliché, but sometimes a visual presentation is worth a thousand words.

3. Improve interpersonal connectedness

People benefit when you talk *with* as opposed to *at* them. They also benefit by talking with each other. Better attention, better learning, better impact. You get rehired.

4. Include a remote executive or subject matter expert

Time and expense are prohibitive if you want someone else to join you on a physical stage. Not so when it's a virtual stage.

5. Save travel time

This not only applies to you (what will you do with all that extra time?), but for every single participant who joins you. This is HUGE, in the benefit department.

6. Save on audio conferencing costs

My friends in the telecom industry will hate me for saying this, but a professional web conferencing platform can (should!) become the starting place for remote communications. Some web conferencing providers let you use all the audio conferencing you want for one flat fee. Powerful.

7. Decrease cancellation and rescheduling disruption

Often cancellations or reschedules are unrecoverable time wasters. Or imagine it takes you 30 minutes to drive to a one-hour coaching session and 30 minutes to get back. By holding a web coaching session, you just recovered 50% of that time cost, but then if they were to cancel…you lose little time, other than what it takes to reschedule.

8. Create new opportunities that didn't exist

This could be the possibility of having a real interaction with someone, or it could be new possibilities for pricing/packaging/positioning in your go-to-market strategy. The "death of distance" for real-time aural, visual, and video (facial) communication will add something irreplaceable to your communications mix.

The final thought

I encourage you to think strategically here. Sometimes what you give up (e.g., actually meeting face-to-face, networking opportunities) and what you get in return (e.g., ability to deliver more presentations in a day or…) aren't in the same category, but the *value equation* is still in your favor.

FOUR REASONS WHY SOME VENDORS HAVE MORE THAN ONE PLATFORM

If you're speaking to an in-person audience, you understand intuitively things such as the differences between communicating to five vs fifty vs five hundred people, and the importance of different seating arrangements, etc. Online this is true, too, but it's one of the most overlooked issues in the web conferencing industry.

1. Organizations have more meetings than events or classes

This is why all web conferencing vendors have platforms made for meetings, but often don't have something designed for webinars or classes.

2. Behaviorally, presentations and classes are different than meetings

Example: in a meeting, all participants are co-equal. Online (in a meeting platform) they start with all audio lines open. In a seminar, they're not. Online (in a webinar) they start with their audio line muted. And trust me, there are a zillion more differences.

3. Training and facilitation tends to be the most complex use case

It's a smaller overall market and exactly the reason that most platform vendors don't have training-oriented products/configurations. Example: a "breakout session" where a large group splits into smaller groups is very much a facilitation-oriented activity. If you're doing training, however, it can be a critical part of facilitating learning—and is entirely missing if you use a meeting-oriented platform.

4. No platform has "all the features" or "is the best"—there is only "best for you"

A few platforms come close to meeting multi-purpose requirements, but you probably wouldn't want to use an "everything but the kitchen sink" platform. Why? You'd lose ease-of-use (which should rank highly on your list of values, whether you realize it or not).

The final thought

Most frequently people just don't know that options like breakout rooms exist. Often when people complain about limitations with web conferencing, it's because they're not using the right tool for the job.

FOUR REASONS VIRTUAL PRESENTATIONS AND CLASSES SHOULD CHANGE THE WAY YOU DESIGN

If you took a speech and put it in a book, you'd instinctively under-stand that the nature of delivering the same impact would require adapting to the medium of communication. Moving an in-person presentation or class to a live, online version requires adaptation, too (though some of it might be less obvious).

1. You should rely on webcam video for connection more than attention

Webcam video has no lateral motion. Unlike an in-person presenter who (most of the time) moves back and forth, a participant's view of a webcam is stationary. Also, Hollywood increases visual stimulation with "camera cuts" (e.g., changes between cameras or scenes), which obviously you don't have with a webcam.

2. Your slides are more important online

The old adage "you are the presentation and your slides are simply support" is less true online. Why? One, your slides are the thing that has the chance to introduce change and visual stimulation into the equation (read: cut through the reticular activating system). Two, the visual real estate of the typical web conferencing platform means slides are much bigger than your webcam video.

3. Your voice is more important online

Two different, multi-hundred person surveys I've done corroborate this. There's more focus on how you use your voice, presumably again because of the change in sensory inputs as compared to in-person communication.

4. Your interactions are going to have to change

Activity, versus passivity, is a critical element of engagement and adult learning. Besides adapting how *you* interact with participants, you'll need to be purposeful about redesigning how you connect participants with each other socially. For example, how do you have participants turn to their neighbor to say hello or work on something together. It's not done in most public webinars, but that doesn't mean that you can't do it—you just have a different set of tools to adapt that interaction to and through.

The final thought

Engagement is multi-dimensional, and rethinking what you do at the sensory, cognitive, and social levels relative to the medium will help you adapt—if not create brand new—ways of connecting and engaging with remote participants.

SEVEN STRATEGIES FOR THINKING BEYOND A SINGLE WEBINAR OR CLASS

A series of webinars or classes has its own unique set of opportunities, many of which are *only* possible when more than one session is involved. The following list of comparisons is far from exhaustive, but it should jumpstart your idea for how to 1) see series differently and 2) creatively capitalize on them. Here's what a series can do:

1. Better enables an overall strategy

Most organizational initiatives such as content marketing programs or educational classes are complex and multifaceted. Single webinars tend to be one-offs. In a series, different sessions can serve different objectives.

2. Frees you up to use different presentation/class styles

A webinar is 45 minutes of presentation and then Q&A at the end, right? That's as much baloney as saying there's only one way to write a book. There's a time for thought-leadership presentations and other times for sales demos. There's a time for an instructor doing most of the talking and a time to facilitate group dialogue. Single sessions risk being "one size fits all."

3. Enables you to create promotional or educational momentum

Every session is a chance to promote the next, and I promise you your response rates will be better than a cold email blast. In educational contexts, you've got the chance to spread out curricula and activities more like a college course would unfold.

4. Makes it easier to be hyper-specific topically

In a single session, it's easy to try to cover too much content. Further, it's harder to tell which part of that content really resonated with the audience. Try a series or multiple sessions where each one is hyper-specific and pay attention to how people respond.

5. Spreads out your risk

Your financial planner usually tells you not to put all investments into a single stock, right? Despite the best planning and research, you don't always get it right. One session often comes with the "all eggs in one basket" pressure, whereas a series mitigates that.

6. Makes it possible to see trends in your efforts

Do a single webinar or class, and can you extrapolate that your invitation response rates (or any other metrics) are what you'll always get? You shouldn't. With a series you'll not only see averages that may be more accurate, you'll be able to see trends to show how you've improved (or not), and occasionally you'll have a blockbuster or dud that is its own learning experience relative to the other sessions in the series.

7. Enables better audience profiling

Whether you're generating leads or profiling learners, a single session always comes with the same pressure to reduce the number of fields of information you ask for on the registration page (to improve response rates). In a strategically planned series, however, you can profile (and better serve audience members over time—especially as their trust in you grows.

The final thought

There's almost always a business reason or organizational objective that's bigger than you as the presenter or facilitator. You may or may not be the person whose job it is to collect and analyze data (or any other aspect of a series mentioned here), but your value only increases when you can be part of (if not lead) the dialogue.

CHAPTER 2

Preparing to Present Virtually

SEVEN IDEAS FOR DEALING WITH DISPARATE GEOGRAPHIC TIME ZONES

Presenting online means, almost by definition, that participants will have a different relationship to the clock than you do. If your goal is to make it easy for them to connect and participate (it is!), consider these tips.

1. Decide whose time zone is more important—yours or theirs

Ten a.m. in your time zone is convenient for you. Ten p.m. in their time zone is convenient for them. If you're a celebrity and they want to stay up late, good for you. For the rest of us, we have to ask if we're willing to be inconvenienced to better serve our clients.

2. When planning, prioritize which additional time zones are important to you

Your first priority is to interact—in real time—with participants who attend your live event. When you think about how they're distributed geographically, who's most important for you to include? Example: If

I want to include an audience in Australia, I can plan a start time in the afternoon (for me in the western United States), but it's almost guaranteed nobody in Europe will show up.

3. Always express start times with time zones

Saying that the session starts at 10 a.m. without including "BDT" (or your equivalent) creates more work for the potential participant. This is a shift when you're used to location-based events that are, by definition, always located in one time zone.

4. When appropriate, include a time zone converter in communications

Better platforms will auto-translate your time zone to be local for participants. Depending on your situation, however, you still may find it useful to include a link to www.timeanddate.com (or equivalent) when you communicate about your event (i.e., in a blog post).

5. Consider repeating the same session multiple times

The time consuming part of a presentation isn't *doing* it, it's *preparing*. Duplicate sessions spaced hours apart will accommodate a bigger chunk of the world. Bonus: use the "copy previous webinar" function in your platform to save a LOT of time.

6. Double-check your own time zone conversion right before the session

Being late to an event you're speaking at isn't cool. Besides checking time zones when you take or create the gig, check right before. (A day in advance? A few hours in advance?) Why? Different places deal with daylight savings time differently (e.g., what is usually an eight hour time difference might be seven hours different for a couple weeks). Don't rely on a reminder from the web conferencing platform alone.

7. Take your time-zone literacy with you

I use TimeScroller on my iPhone, but you can do this with native apps on both iOS and Android devices. It's not always because I'm traveling, but because it's the fastest way to be sure.

The final thought

Presenting virtually totally changes up how you relate to time and place. That you don't have to travel and can reach new participants is obvious, but it's no fun to accidentally be late because your time zone changed and theirs didn't or you're not used to translating time zones in your head. The fix is easy; you've just got to be aware and go do it.

EIGHT STRATEGIES FOR DEALING WITH WIDELY VARYING COMPUTING ENVIRONMENTS

As a presenter or trainer you know that the effectiveness of your session is more than simply delivering content. You have to consider the user experience with a device, and ideally you consider their social experience with you and others in the session. In other words, you're the leader who will be guiding producers, promoters, and moderators to better understand and execute on behalf of the audience.

1. Decide your "lowest common denominator" of inclusiveness

Optimizing a participant's experience comes from awareness of the finer details of *their* access to your session (e.g., monitor size/resolution, computer vs mobile version of the platform you're using, operating systems, etc.). Accommodating everyone, regardless of the device they're joining with may require you to leave out an option available to you.

2. Choose a technology or setting that works better with lower bandwidths

This is a specialized version of the previous point. I'm guessing you'll have little choice about choosing a different platform based on this requirement, but you can make design/planning choices that use less bandwidth (e.g., having your slides look okay in 8-bit/256 colors instead of millions, finding an alternative to the video you were going to use, etc.).

37

3. Offer participants an option to dial in by telephone

VoIP doesn't actually take that much bandwidth, but there are other reasons why you might be sure to include a phone-in option. One is because sometimes people are going to join when a full computing environment isn't possible (like listening in while they're driving). Another is because sometimes VoIP is blocked or less-than-friendly with firewalls. Yet another is because this provides a backup for attendance if connectivity is an issue and the web conference is experiencing latency.

Remember, too, that sometimes the choices you provide are for behavioral, not technical, reasons. I've had folks who want to dial in on the telephone because they could listen privately or quietly versus having their computer speakers on.

4. Use a participant guide (made available in advance)

A participant guide, worksheet, or the equivalent can be a powerful addition to the experience. Many people benefit greatly by being able to take notes as they go, and if they're on telephone alone (without the web/video conference), they'll still feel involved.

5. Plan multiple slides instead of using animations, screen-sharing, or video

I'm wrapping a number of issues and solutions into one answer here, but they're all resolved tactically with approaching the medium a little differently. Plan multiple/additional slides instead of relying on how your web conferencing solution handles PowerPoint animations (results do vary) or as a backup to doing a live desktop demo or using a video (in case of connectivity issues).

6. Employ a skilled moderator

A great moderator or co-facilitator makes presenters better than they are alone. This might be because 1) the presenter/facilitator is more confident and engaging, 2) the moderator can handle issues as they arise in a way the presenter can't or doesn't want to, or 3) they have the experience to know what to do if something really goes wrong so the session is salvaged (if not useful).

7. Serve the broader group first

If anyone experiences a technical problem, it's almost always something that they alone are experiencing. It's just a fact of life when participants have different computing devices, different vendors for connectivity, different organizational rules that govern how and when they access the web, different levels of experience, and on and on.

You want everyone to be able to participate, and it's particularly painful to feel like you're letting someone down. Remember, though, that if you stop to handle one person, everyone else is waiting and being held up. Troubleshoot with individuals as you can, but not at the expense of the group.

8. Publish requirements/limitations in advance . . . repeatedly

If you know your audience isn't going to be able to participate with a particular operating system or browser or whatever, put that in the pre-session communications. If you want to be particularly vigilant, send out an extra email that doesn't have the ignore-ability of your platform's system-generated reminders.

Finally, give yourself a bit of grace. People are busy, and they don't read this stuff. Swallow hard, change their diapers, and move on.

The final thought

If all of the above sounds a little overwhelming, remember this: this book is for the intermediate or advanced user. It's okay (and not a showstopper) if something here doesn't fit you and where you're at. You'll grow into it. I promise you don't need to become a techie, just someone who asks better questions.

FIVE REASONS TO START TAKING YOUR OWN PICTURES FOR PRESENTATIONS

Excellent stock imagery isn't cheap, and most organizations have limited budgets for such investments. Even if you do have a budget, there are several compelling reasons to start capturing your own imagery.

1. They're free

My bookkeeper once calculated that I've invested more than $6500 in stock imagery. The good news is that it's quality stuff and I can re-use them, but I've managed to cut a big chunk of that budget by taking my own photos.

2. You're the best person to tell your story

Your own pictures are naturally going to be from your point of view. And who else has a front row seat to seeing life the way you do?

3. You'll develop your eye for telling stories with pictures

As you grow from "taking snapshots" to "telling stories," you'll start seeing how visuals relate to points that you want to make.

4. You've probably got a "good enough" camera in your phone

Unless you need high-gloss print quality, the camera in your phone is adequate for presentations. Or, good quality point-and-shoot digital cameras don't cost a lot these days, and you may have one of those too.

5. You'll be distinctive and build your own brand

Every one of us—even if you work inside an organization—needs to continually create unique value. Anyone can share your facts, but no one can tell your story the way you can.

The final thought

Nobody sees the world like you do. That's a good thing. It's an entirely exploitable thing, and as someone once quipped, "Anyone can share your facts, but nobody can tell your story." A webinar or virtual class is a perfect place to do that visually, and getting in the habit of capturing and using your own photos is not only easy, it's distinctive.

NINE THOUGHTS ABOUT TAKING YOUR OWN PICTURES FOR YOUR PRESENTATIONS

You're convinced you should start shooting your own pictures. Here are a few lessons I've learned along the way.

1. Shoot for story before quality

Your presentation is to get people to think, feel, or do something (or all three). Growing from amateur to pro means learning to go beyond decorating slides to advancing your message.

2. Shoot multiple shots from various angles and compositions

You spend no money to shoot several shots in the same fell swoop. Place the object of the picture in various positions (top one third, bottom one third, whatever). You'll have more flexibility when cropping the image later. The same goes with capturing multiple angles if you can. Parallel to both of these is zooming (telescopically). Shoot something closer up and farther away.

3. Save the editing for the laptop

Yes, I know filters and effects can be fun. In most cases, though, your phone isn't a great substitute for seeing the picture in the context of a presentation. Wait to do the editing.

4. Always save the original file

Often a picture has more than one story to tell. Don't leave part of a story on the cutting room floor (how's that for an analog analogy for a digital "thang"?).

5. Name the image usefully

I embed keywords right into the file name so I can find it in a search of my computer. Trust me, when you're putting a presentation together it's a momentum-killer to slog through 732 files visually because they are all named something like IMG_123.

6. Create a special library for your work

If you have a large quantity of images, you'll save a lot of time if you have a file dedicated to those you use professionally or on a particular topic. This is especially true if you've named the file poorly and they're buried in the midst of all those pictures of Uncle Joe's "Got-my-bunion-removed" party.

7. Be legally wise

This is the fine print that says that I don't render legal or professional advice and you should consult your attorney, doctor, and shaman before engaging in any program of this kind. Gag. We all live in different worlds professionally. Just be aware that your organization's legal counsel may have an opinion about this kind of stuff.

8. Consider carrying a model release form

You can find examples on the web or your organization may have one. You may not need it, but it's probably better to not discover that you can't use an awesome pic because you didn't get someone who's in it to sign a waiver. It's generally not illegal to take a picture of someone in a public place (assuming you're not doing something lewd), but carrying a release form is a way to circumvent future issues if it's a concern to you.

9. Cite yourself in the image credits

You're building your cred as uniquely valuable. We should give credit to others when we use their work, but don't overlook giving yourself the same.

The final thought

I was speaking to a group once and someone objected, "I don't have time for another project." I think the statement was fair, but here's why I think it's also shortsighted: nobody has time for a project, but most all of us have our phones (cameras) with us all day long. Success will be had when you change your *habit*, but then that's true for spotting and collecting stories, opportunities to make a new business connection, and many other things. Don't make a project out of it, make capturing your world visually a habit.

THREE STEPS FOR ADAPTING IN-PERSON ACTIVITIES TO ONLINE

When virtual presentations and classes are lackluster, often it's because we lose the natural interactions that happen in in-person settings. It doesn't have to be that way. The change of medium of communication does change things, and we first notice what we lose before we notice what we gain. These three steps will ease your path.

1. Analyze what you do in an in-person presentation or class

Consider each thing you do with an in-person audience. How do you kick things off? Where do you plan interactions or exercises? Do you use on-the-fly interactions such as *"Raise your hand if you like ice cream."* Then, consider how to translate these things using your online platform.

2. Map your tactics to your platform's tools

Many in-person tactics will directly translate to a feature in your platform (e.g., "raise hand"). Some, however, won't. Get creative with figuring out alternative ways to adapt your in-person activities for online participants.

3. Discover what you can do better or different in the new medium (your web conferencing platform)

Example: imagine you ask fifteen people in a class to share their names and what they like to do on a weekend. In person this may take fifteen minutes because responses are sequential. Doing the same thing online in a group chat area would take a minute or two because it's simultaneous.

The final thought

To say that anything you can do offline can be translated online would be irresponsible, but as I noted, you'll discover things you can do online that are superior, perhaps even unique relative to in-person presentations and classes. For an awesome chart about adapting in-person stuff to online, go to the Extras web page, log in, and grab the "How to Translate Your In-Person Presentations Online" paper (remember, the URL and password are in the How to Get the Most out of This Book part of this book).

SIX SLIDE "GOTCHAS" TO WATCH OUT FOR

Web conferencing platforms deal with slides differently. You don't have to worry as much if you're just sharing slides from your computer desktop ("screen sharing"), but many platforms prefer you to "upload" your slides. If how your slides look is important to you, pay attention to the following.

1. Determine if you can use something besides PowerPoint

Nearly all platforms that upload (read: convert) your slides are not friendly to Keynote, Prezi, Google Slides, or other alternatives you may be using.

2. Plan to test your slides well in advance

The conversion process may not play nice with graphics, gradient colors, etc. You don't want to figure this out as you're walking on stage.

3. Plan to look through all your slides in the green room before going onstage

"Green room" is a holdover phrase from how television studios or theaters work. They function as a waiting room before people go on stage, and somewhere in history they were painted green. It has many uses in the virtual world, including checking that your slides are all uploaded—and it gets messier. Some platforms that convert slides are inconsistent at it, so what worked a week ago may not work so well today. It's not common, but it happens.

4. Check the resolution settings of the room

Some platforms default to lower-than-awesome resolution, and the settings are changed at the room level (for each session, not usually globally). This might mean that a shape with a gradient color looks weird or a marginal image now looks awful.

5. Consider multiple slides instead of animations

Better platforms support PowerPoint animations, but you still have a problem: the least reliable part of a participant's experience is their own connection to a local internet service provider. Animations that look smooth on your end still could be wonky for them. Easy fix: use multiple slides to accomplish the same effect.

6. Be ready for upload/conversion times

I often use a lot of high-resolution images which means that my deck can be fifty-plus megabytes. Don't learn too late that your platform's going to take twenty minutes to convert your deck.

The final thought

There's an old behind-the-scenes saying in the software industry: "If you want perfect software, are you willing to pay for it?" And that saying was around even before people thought they were getting ripped off for a two dollar phone app. The only antidote for the occasional idiosyncrasies in web conferencing platforms (or any software, really) is agility. If something happens just breathe, roll with it, and make a note for next time.

SIX IDEAS FOR WHEN YOU *HAVE* TO PUT ALL THAT TEXT ON A SLIDE

Most of us are fans of visual, minimal-text, context-building, storytelling slides. In reality, however, sometimes you have to just put a pile of text on a slide (e.g., to teach a legal definition or review specific wording for some marketing copy). In a webinar this is problematic because, unlike a book, it's harder for a viewer to adjust so they can see more clearly.

1. Ask, "Where do the eyes go?"

When someone first glances at the slide, where do you want them to look first? Hint: White space (or "negative space") is your friend.

2. Pay attention to font size

Hopefully you do this for an in-person room, too (so participants in the back row can see it). Online you may have mobile attendees with smaller screens. It is likely your online participants can't zoom or change resolution on the fly.

3. Increase line spacing

In PowerPoint (or your equivalent), "line spacing" is the distance between lines of text. More space will help a pile of text look less crammed.

4. Be careful with highlights

To make text stand out, it's tempting to overuse bold, italicized, or colored text. Remember, if too much is accented, nothing stands out.

5. Consider a participant guide

Maybe not everything needs to go on the slide. Using a physical/printed participant guide serves many purposes, including making it easier for someone to read your swath of text.

6. Create a sequence with a series of slides

There is no rule that you need to have few slides. Create one slide with your text, duplicate it, and then highlight passages of text sequentially to guide the reading experience.

The final thought

Putting a lot of text on slides is not usually preferable, but it's also not a mortal sin. In fact, when you raise your level of consciousness about it (especially those of you who really do have to use swaths of text in your profession), you *can* improve the effectiveness of your communication *and* actually have your audience appreciate how you did it.

FIVE IDEAS FOR SHARING SOMETHING BESIDES POWERPOINT ON YOUR DESKTOP

When you present or train online, anything on your computer desktop is fair game. In fact, it's powerful for you to drop out of full screen PowerPoint mode to demonstrate something from your desktop—participants get an "over your shoulder" view and the change-up is good visual stimulus.

1. Make sure all pop-up notifications are turned off

The last thing you need is getting an instant message from your significant other saying, *"Yo, hottie, looking forward to tonight."* I'm not kidding. It happens.

2. Plan your story or key points when presenting

Love it or hate it, PowerPoint forces you to present in a linear way (unless you're purposeful about doing something else). Commonly, though, presenters start wandering in a way that's counter to clear communication. Know what you're going to say and show.

3. Plan your sharing style according to the purpose of your presentation

If the presentation is formal, be clear and to the point. If it's less formal (such as a small-group software demonstration), it's okay to be more conversational, perhaps even adjusting what you show based on participant questions.

4. Have what you're going to show prepared

Instead of wasting time navigating to a website, have it already loaded in a browser tab. Instead of wasting time typing passwords and logging into a system you're going to show, be logged in already.

5. Pause your screen sharing if you need to navigate someplace private

Remember that your desktop is live in front of everyone. Pausing your screen share freezes participants' view until you un-pause, allowing you to navigate someplace (such as to retrieve something else to show). Don't forget to un-pause (duh!).

The final thought

The awesomeness of being able to have an audience "look over your shoulder at your desktop" cannot be understated. The movement creates visual interestingness, and I promise you will differentiate yourself from all those "talk over PowerPoint" webinars and classes.

SIX THINGS WE KNOW FROM POWERPOINT RESEARCH YOU CAN APPLY

The body of empirical research about PowerPoint is relatively small. Here are a few ideas, however, that will positively impact the power of your slides to communicate in a webinar, webcast, or virtual class.

1. Show the whole before the parts

This study specifically looked at animations, in the context of flying, in bullet points one-by-one and found that this actually hurt recall. Generally, the brain needs structure or context before diving into the details.

If all the bullet points form a cohesive whole, show the whole first (even if you break it down subsequently to speak to each bullet in more detail). Even if they aren't a "whole," consider using bullet points like headlines.

Mahar, Steve, Ulku Yaylacicegi, and Thomas N. Janicki. "Less is More When Developing PowerPoint Animations." Information Systems Education Journal Vol. 7, no. 82 (2009): 1-11.

2. Use visuals to explain the difficult, complex, or abstract

This study evaluated the use of PowerPoint relative to a traditional classroom lecture that otherwise used whiteboard/chalkboard/flip-chart for explaining physics (arguably, for most of us, a complex topic). While the author posits that simple text is fine for declarative statements, PowerPoint improved comprehension, likely through the improved ability to represent meaningful information more easily.

Ask yourself if the topic is sufficiently difficult, complex, or abstract you could more easily "show" than "tell." If the answer is "yes," how might you show it (e.g., build a diagram with shapes, use a photo that expresses the idea, etc.)?

Erdemir, Naki. "The Effect of PowerPoint and Traditional Lectures on Students' Achievement in Physics." Journal of Turkish Science Education Vol. 8, no. 3 (2011): 176-189.

3. Use sans serif fonts for optimum professionalism

This study evaluated ten common fonts, five serif and five sans serif, asking participants to evaluate them on four qualities: 1) comfortable-to-read, 2) professionalism, 3) interesting, and 4) attractiveness. Only one, professionalism, demonstrated statistically significant differentiation. The highest rated font overall was Gill Sans.

You may or may not get to choose your fonts. If so, consider using three or fewer for the whole presentation. One common combination is to use a sans serif font for the main/body text and a serif font for headlines.

Mackiewicz, Jo. "Audience Perceptions of Fonts in Projected PowerPoint Text Slides." Technical Communication Vol. 54, no. 3 (2007): 295-307.

4. Use a complete idea in the slide's title

This study evaluated content recall on slides with differing approaches to titles (short, incomplete descriptions versus complete sentences). The group seeing slides with complete sentences in the title had far better recall than the group seeing more "typical" slide titles.

I extrapolate this to a "complete idea" rather than "complete sentence," but the key is that this is the main point of the slide. If you have two key points to make, consider two slides (even if the slide is the same). Remember, your content (how long you talk) determines your speech's duration, not the number of slides you have. Many PowerPoint templates have exceedingly large fonts for the title space...you may need to adjust to improve your impact.

Alley, Michael, and Kathryn A. Neely. "Discovering the Power of PowerPoint: Rethinking the Design of Presentation Slides from a Skillful User's Perspective." Proceedings of the 2005 American Society for Engineering Education Annual Conference and Exposition (American Society for Engineering Education, 2005).

5. Use relevant visuals...or skip them

This study looked at the use of photographs in presentations, but I think the results have broader implications. The study tested photos that were decorative vs. complementary, and it did so with and without audio narration. The study found that the most significant factor for comprehension was a photo that was complementary (added something to understanding). Of note, presentations with narration were best at keeping attention.

I'll argue here that I think this would be true of any visual that is complementary. It takes work, but take the time to find or create a visual that helps understanding, memory, and, perhaps, your persuasiveness. Avoid "decoration." Images used simply to beautify actually hurt the cause...the viewer has to work to figure out what it means (or doesn't).

Slykhuis, David A., Eric N. Wiebe, and Len A. Annetta. "Eye-Tracking Students' Attention to PowerPoint Photographs in a Science Education Setting." Journal of Science Education and Technology, Vol. 14, Nos. 5/6, December 2005.

6. Format graphs for message and aesthetics

This study examined if participants could accurately extract information from graphs presented in 2D or 3D with different color hues or solid black and white. Overall, 2D graphs led to better comprehension, particularly when complex information was presented. Accuracy was similar for color and black and white.

Focus on "meaning making." The study authors didn't rule out ever using a 3D graph, but they warned that the dimensionality should be related to "meaning making" (or it would be extraneous). Avoid extraneous anything. The study didn't evaluate labels or other chart/graph elements, but other trusted sources suggest that anything not critical to the essential message has a chance to hurt you.

Stewart, Brandie M., Jessica M. Cipolla, and Lisa A. Best. "Extraneous Information and Graph Comprehension: Implications for Effective Design Choices." Campus-Wide Information Systems Vol. 26, no. 3 (2009): 191-200.

The final thought

The research cited here was all done specific to Microsoft PowerPoint. You can and should, however, extrapolate this to include Keynote, Prezi, or perhaps even more generally "visual learning." Given that slides play such a big role in webinars and virtual classes, though, the takeaway is that we can make easy, small changes to improve attention and impact. Well, that and the fact that many or most organizations institutionalize crappy presentation practices, but we'll save that editorializing for another time.

TWO ESSENTIAL PRINCIPLES FOR GREAT POLLS

Polls are one of the most powerful forms of interactivity in a virtual room. Why? Because not only do they involve active participation, but the results are captured in reporting. Done well, they're not only engaging during your presentation, but yield quantifiable intelligence.

1. Use a poll when it's the right tool for the interaction

Not every interaction belongs in a poll. Sometimes you don't need multiple-choice responses, and sometimes you simply need a quick show of hands. A poll takes fractionally longer to conduct than, "put up your hand if…" Still other times you'd be better off gathering qualitative feedback (such as typed chat responses).

2. Think, "extend the dialogue" instead of "be interactive"

Polls are tools for asking questions. Don't be interactive because someone said you should—ask questions that advance your message and get people thinking. The most engaging thing you can do is ask a great question versus just being interactive because some ding-a-ling like me said you should be.

The final thought

Ultimately, talking *with* people instead of *at* them isn't just a webinar or virtual class problem, it's a social shift. Even in the offline world of speaking and teaching, people are waking up to the fact that there is a decreased tolerance for lecture or monologues as communication (it has its place, but it's been overused). Polling tools in web conferencing solutions are one of the most powerful and versatile features, and I give them extra space here because they're *better* online than in-person.

FOUR TIPS FOR WRITING A BRAIN-FRIENDLY POLL OR TEST QUESTION

Using a platform's polling or testing function is easy. The hard part is writing a great question that is stimulating and makes sense. Here are a few guidelines to help you dial 'em in.

1. Write the "stem" so it could be answered without the choices

In official lingo, the stem is the question or statement that leads up to the multiple choices. I hope it goes without saying that it should focus on only one clearly formulated problem. Test your question by covering up the answers. Ask yourself, "Could the poll-taker understand and answer the question?"

2. Put most of the wording in the stem

Your objective should be to minimize how many times the attendee or learner has to read each item. Make it easy for them to read the stem one time and the answers as few times as possible.

3. Keep all answer options parallel and grammatically consistent

Inconsistency makes the brain work harder. We do want attendees or learners to have to think (it's critical for engagement and learning), but we don't want them churning brain cycles figuring out something that's poorly written.

4. Write answers so they don't unintentionally give away clues to the correct answer

Is the length of the correct answer in proportion? Is there a verbal or idiomatic clue that relates the answer to the stem? Are the "distractors" (wrong answers) plausible? Are the answers in an order that may give something away?

Some ideas for taking action include making sure there isn't a word association that gives it away, stimulating thought by ensuring the distractors are reasonably logical choices, and/or arranging the answers in alphabetical or numerical order.

The final thought

Want to brush up on parallel structure? There's a fabulous reminder here: https://owl.english.purdue.edu/owl/resource/623/1/. Too, see the "poor" and "better" examples below.

Well-written polls enhance engagement and learning

Poor: The AIDA marketing model is:
   A. the latest thinking in marketing
   B. only works with small business
   C. a list of potential steps or points of discovery in getting a customer to buy
   D. converts list members into buyers

Better: The third step in the AIDA marketing model stands for:
   A. Demand
   B. Desire
   C. Destination
   D. Determination

TheVirtualPresenter.com

FIVE ADVANCED POLL-PLANNING TACTICS

Dynamic dialogue with an online audience isn't hard, but it is different. When you're ready for the next step, consider these additional tactics for planning to engage participants.

1. Combine polls with questions or chat to overcome platform limitations

Most web conferencing solutions limit the number of multiple choice answers you can use (e.g., you have eight potential answers and your conferencing platform limits you to five). Solution: list the first four and make the fifth answer, "Other (please ask a question to share your response)."

2. Combine polls with questions or chat to catch "long tail" responses

Sometimes the potential responses to your question are numerous, but you know the typical or most frequent responses. Solution: list the frequent responses as the polling responses, and like the immediately preceding point, use questions or chat to bat cleanup on the rest.

3. Use polls as mini-research projects by trying a Likert scale

A Likert scale is a common and easy-to-use tactic in surveys, but we rarely see them in webinar polls. For shame! Make each response numeric, but label the scale so it is easy to understand. Example: 1 – Strongly Disagree, 2, 3 – Neither Agree or Disagree, 4, 5 – Strongly Agree.

4. Use polls as mini-research projects by crowdsourcing ideas for the future

Done right, your dialogue with your marketplace can give you the feedback that helps you dial in future content or messaging. It's seriously faster than setting up a survey on the web and trying to drive response. Bonus: use this as an opportunity to soft-promote the next webinar or class, too.

5. Build placeholder slides into your presentation deck

In the heat of the moment, it's easy to forget where you were going to activate the poll. Use a slide in your presentation deck as a placeholder. You won't be able to miss it, and it will help you better plan the flow of the presentation. Note that this assumes you've gotten over the idea that your slide deck is a great handout, because someone looking at your deck as a *document* is going to wonder why you wasted space in their printout).

The final thought

Let's go a little deeper on Point #4 as an example. Imagine your poll says, "Of the following list, which are most important to you when <fill in the blank>." Great! Now you have an idea not only for the content of the next session, but key words to use when promoting it, too. But now when you *deliver* the poll, in that few seconds while you're waiting for people to vote, you could casually mention the date and time for that next session (perhaps even sharing a link). Your only limit with polling is your own willingness to get creative. Let 'er rip.

CHAPTER 3

Collaborating with Participants, Promoters, & Presenters

SIX RELATIONSHIPS EVERY VIRTUAL PRESENTER OR TRAINER SHOULD CULTIVATE

A book that looks at beyond-the-basics ideas for presenters and facilitators wouldn't be complete without looking at other roles involved with executing virtual events, classes, and programs.

1. **The *Presenter* (that's you) creates and delivers participant experiences**

I call this out for two reasons: you have a role *and a responsibility* to be the thought leader in getting beyond talking-head or talking-over-PowerPoint experiences. You're the one who will push the envelopes (and buttons?) of others who've never seen a webinar or class delivered like you are going to. Your first relationship is to your own expectations of what a webinar or virtual class is versus what it could be.

2. Attendee, participant, learner, delegate

However you refer to them (and I use all of them), the days of "show up and throw up" are quickly fading into the past. Part of the relationship is the presentation or class itself, but part is what happens before and after (e.g., conversations in the hallway). Want to be an influencer? Think beyond the presentation or class.

3. The *Producer* sets up and manages the technology

A great presentation with many attendees fails when something doesn't work in the participant-experience category. The Producer not only manages production, but often is the person who acts as the project planner or lead. They're the go-to person to talk to about what's possible when you're planning and adapting your session.

4. The *Promoter* plans and delivers on getting butts in seats

A great presentation and production fails when nobody shows up (or they show up with wrong expectations). The Promoter owns the myriad of options for messaging and media associated with generating interest and getting people to take action. They're the go-to person to talk to about the nuances that will turn into a zillion tweets, registration page copy, etc.

5. The *Moderator* is the emcee, color commentator, and yin to your yang

This assumes you have a yang, of course. Amateur moderators are going to deliver a welcome script and introduce you. That adds no value. Good ones, though, will never steal your thunder and, at the same time, make you better than you are.

6. The *Instructional Designer* plans and designs curricula

Classic instructional design is focused on content and performance measurement. This isn't wrong. A small-but-growing number of ID pros, however, are realizing that designing instruction for a *live* virtual class also has a performance element beyond how to create a lot of PowerPoint slides. These people are gold, because they'll help you design interactions and cognitive ticklers that will totally differentiate your class.

The final thought

To be fair, I could or should write a whole *set* of books based on the related roles and perspectives above, but who wants to read a 500-page book about webinars? There's some level of learning that really should move from a book to a conversation with a consultant (I know many consultants, if you decide you hate me and want a recommendation).

SIX TIPS FOR A PROJECT KICKOFF MEETING

Getting ready for a virtual presentation is a team activity, but I'll assume you're taking a leadership role. You may not formally "own" the session or leadership thereof, but experientially you'll find many people who don't really have any more experience doing virtual presentations than you do. Effectively kicking off your webinar or virtual class project will save you a pile of headache down the road—and, especially if you intend to push the envelope with style or content, you need to have everyone on the same page. Here are some things to think about.

1. Conduct the meeting with video conferencing—even if you're all in the same building

The fastest way to get people (all of them) more comfortable with your platform's tools is to do it in the "room" you'll be using for the presentation or class. Bonus: use the *webinar or training platform* you intend to use for the presentation/class you're planning (versus the *meeting platform*).

2. Don't treat the project kickoff meeting as a training session

A kickoff meeting will often involve a fairly broad audience. Keep it short and focused on the key elements of your event. Save the heavy details for later. Not everyone needs the same type or level of training on the web conferencing platform.

3. **At a minimum, establish expectations, timelines, roles, and dependencies.**

Use this meeting to establish or confirm three things: 1) top-level expectations and timelines (why, what, when), 2) roles and dependencies (who), and 3) team member's contact information and preferred contact method (how).

4. **Review key milestones against the calendars of team members**

Vacations, holidays, team retreats, other organizational initiatives, and a hundred other things may interfere with deadlines and milestones. Don't figure out at the eleventh hour that a key team member can't do a technical walkthrough because they're at the dentist.

5. **Avoid brainstorming**

Avoid time-wasting confusion. "Wait, I thought someone said....?" Oy. If some part of the team needs to figure something out, suggest they 'parking lot' the issue and establish the appropriate time for sharing the results with the group.

6. **End the project kickoff meeting early**

Nobody ever complains about a meeting ending early, but there's another valuable reason to do it. Someone should make sure the meeting summary or minutes gets effectively distributed (an online project management tool like Podio is waaay better than email). This'll give you time to do it.

The final thought

With a tight agenda and a focused kickoff meeting that ends early, you will subtly communicate to the team that your meetings are going to be efficient, increasing the likelihood that you can influence those who do not directly report to you.

EIGHT THINGS THAT BELONG ON YOUR REHEARSAL CHECKLIST

If you want to stand out as a professional, insist on a rehearsal. Or at least a "dry run" or walk through of the session. Here's why: as web conferencing has become more ubiquitous, plenty of people treat it like a phone call (which isn't wrong in certain contexts), but they fail to give an event or class the attention it deserves to ensure everybody's on the same page. A few things to think about:

1. **Use the exact same computer and setup you intend to use for the actual event**

This is technology we're talking about. Stuff happens, usually in a way that seems random (or it could just be sunspots are heavy or there's been a bigfoot sighting). I promise, using the same computer(s), headsets, lighting, and all that is a lot easier to do than figuring something out 30 minutes before the rehearsal.

2. **Test moving your slides, both forward and backward**

Ideally you're as facile and flexible online as you are onsite. Know how to navigate.

3. **Locate and practice using your interactivity tools**

If you have to "think about it" in the middle of a session, the likelihood of you using the extra tools (e.g., drawing or knowing how to launch your poll) are either nil or the process will feel clunky and like you're getting the stare down from a huge, all-seeing eye.

4. Discuss how polls will flow

Will the presenter (you) launch your own poll? If so, do you know how to open, close, and then share the results? If not, who will and what cues will you use so they know when to do that? Will there be a little small talk about something while waiting for responses? Will you share the results with the audience? Discuss the results before moving on?

5. Discuss the logistics of managing text-based Q&A

If more than one person is behind-the-scenes or otherwise involved with questions, how will questions be monitored? Will they all be answered? Verbally or textually? Will the moderator and behind-the-scenes teams split up questions based on type? Will you answer questions *during* the session? If so, will you do it at pre-planned times or on-the-fly?

6. Discuss the logistics of managing audio Q&A

Most of the questions I just identified for text-based Q&A apply to audio (voice), but I call out the latter because it's such a huge opportunity for you to make an impact. Why? Because unless you were delivering a keynote speech, you'd never do an in-person event and make the person who raised their hand wait 'til the end of the session for an answer. Because there are so many crappy talk-at-you events that you'll look like a rock star if you let someone raise their hand, take them off mute, and let them ask their question. Just figure out who will do the muting/unmuting.

7. Figure out your transitions

The biggest place webinars et al. feel clunky is in transitions—somebody kicks it off, introduces the speaker, then you launch a poll and both of you chat, then you close it, discuss it, and you keep presenting. Then a question comes in that the moderator thinks you should answer on the spot. And on and on. Not hard, different. Just know how you'll do those things.

8. Decide if there will be a post-session debrief, and if so, how

A few platforms let the presentation team retreat back into the "green room." More often it's just as easy to use an 'instant meeting' to get everyone together immediately following the session to review what went well and what could be better.

The final thought

You're a professional at something, and you're likely a professional because you did the work. If you treat a webinar, webcast, or virtual class with the appropriate respect, you'll not only deliver a better experience, but that same experience will elicit "wow, I've never been to a webinar like that before" comments. Just be a pro about it.

TWENTY-THREE TIPS TO PASS ALONG TO YOUR PROMOTER

As the presenter, it might not be your personal responsibility to do all the promotion for your session. As a leader, however, you will be the direct beneficiary of getting the message right, getting it through, and getting participants to show up. What follows isn't exhaustive (that'd be a book unto itself), but it does cover many underutilized tactics that you can influence.

Messaging

1. Get your session name to do double duty

When refining what to call your presentation or training, remember that a big chunk of your promotional effort needs to be carried by the name itself (such as on social media). Generally, fancy titles that work for books or conference presentations work less well online.

2. Create a pile of variations of your session's benefits for social media

Doing A/B tests on messages is possible for nearly everyone, but there's an ROI to be done—often the effort doesn't pay off in terms of the return (i.e., improving response rates by 5% when that means a few more attendees might not be worth the effort). A simple way to mitigate risk is to list out the benefits of attending your session, create a bunch of catchy variations, and get to tweeting.

3. Bring the power of "live" to life in your promotional copy

"Join this live, interactive session to learn . . . " is common language for virtual sessions. The problem is that nobody believes it anymore because most of them are more "talking AT you" than "talking WITH you" experiences. Do yourself a favor and tell 'em *how* you'll be different. For example, will there be an extended Q&A session? A promise that every question will get a response? Hands-on exercises? An "ask the expert" approach?

Awareness and invitations

4. Save space in the subject line with your "from" line

The first thing email readers read is the name of who an email came from. Better utilize the "from" line and you'll have more of the limited space in the subject line for content. Example: if you use a company name, use "Company Name Webinars" or the equivalent to eliminate the need to use "webinar" in the subject line.

5. Include the benefit as early as possible in the subject line

How many characters or words are readable in an email client's subject line vary a lot. The best rule of thumb is to wordsmith what you put there so you don't force the goodies out of sight.

6. Choose webinar listing sites with care

Generally people aren't out searching the web for webinars or training sessions to attend. What they do search for is content that's relevant to them. If you do a search for "webinar listing site" you'll find plenty, and they come and go regularly. Why? Most are generic listing services. And remember, even free has a cost—your time.

7. Create a new tag or category on your blog

Posting on your blog that you have a session upcoming is one thing. Having a category or tag that someone could click on to find all of them, future and past, is another.

8. Use "product placement" in your blog posts

Hollywood has figured out that you might pay attention to a character drinking Coke when you don't pay attention to Coke advertising on television. Similarly, you could write a valuable blog post that includes a mention of your upcoming session. Better: position attending your webinar like a no-brainer next step for getting more of the goodness. Best: make sure that once your session is done, that link goes to where readers can access the recording.

9. Use automated emails to promote other sessions

Assuming you've got an awesome platform that allows these emails to be customized, this is a great opportunity to include additional calls-to-action.

10. Capture social media testimonials

If someone says something nice publicly in the New York Times you can quote it. You could do the same with people saying nice things on Twitter (trust me, I have hundreds—it's powerful).

11. Find your unique "other" opportunities

I did a study in 2010 asking people what they used and what worked best for them. Email was number one in both categories, but a surprise finding was the "other" category. The qualitative comments revealed things that were specific to each person's situation. For example, one person said, "We create a message/link to have the sales/service teams append to their email signature." Great idea! Go find yours.

Registration pages

12. DO reiterate your marketing copy, including the benefits of attending

A friend in the media business shared with me some pretty ugly bounce rates (people who don't register once they hit your page). Her suggestion? Don't assume they read the email invitation. And this is even better advice when a social media click-through might have very little information.

13. Think of registration fields as the price of admission

Our temptation is to ask for a lot of information from registrants. This isn't wrong, but the more you ask for, the more potential people will bail out. Only ask for what you really need and/or will use.

14. Use a custom question as a mini-survey

Finding out about the wants, needs, and desires of your audience before they show up is a powerful way to boost your relevance. This assumes, of course, that you look at the information that's been collected and do something with it (don't laugh, most presenters don't).

15. Ask for their Twitter handle or other social media handle

Want to powerfully build your social capital? Don't ask them to connect with you—you connect with them.

16. Redirect registrants to another call-to-action

Once someone completes registering for your session, where do they go? Better platforms let you redirect them anywhere you want them to go. This could be a survey, another webinar, a social media page, or . . . .

Confirmation, reminder, and follow-up emails

17. Customize subject lines to cut through inbox noise

System-generated emails are great at pulling the information entered at setup (which saves you or someone a pile of time). The downside is that that's all they can do. Better platforms let you customize them so you can improve how they appear in someone's inbox.

18. Customize the body of emails to include additional calls-to-action

Join your Facebook group? Connect on Twitter? Forward to a friend? Register for another webinar or download a paper? Your web conferencing solution doesn't have a know-what-I'm-thinking feature (yet), so you'll need to help it out in this department.

19. Send multiple reminders

Two emails are customary for webinar/virtual classroom platforms: a confirmation email that a registrant receives upon completing registration and a reminder. Some systems, though, let you send multiple reminders. Remember, someone has expressed interest and has opted into receiving these—send multiples.

20. Adjust the timing of your reminder emails relative to holidays and weekends

Better platforms let you define how far in advance of the session you want a reminder to be sent (e.g., one week, two days, one hour). Take one additional step to make sure the reminder hits their inbox at a time that increases its likelihood to have an impact.

Follow up tactics

21. Think "quid pro quo" for the handout or other material

Quid pro quo is Latin meaning "what for what." There's no reason to give away the farm just because people want free stuff. Ask them to fill out the exit or post-event survey, like your Facebook page, or whatever.

22. Expire the recording

You read that right. Give it a deadline for the same reason sales at retail stores have deadlines—they motivate action. It might not be the right tactic for every situation, but if your message is timely, just hanging the recording out there in the ether doesn't necessarily solve your problem.

23. Follow up with Tweeters with a personal thank you

To be fair, this is probably something that you, the presenter, should do more often than not. Want to build your tribe? "Hang out in the hallway and talk with people" has always been a solid strategy. Now just do that online.

The final thought

The list of potential tactics is endless, but two things are for certain. One, 100% of those you don't try don't work. Two, your opportunity to differentiate yourself, the organization you're presenting or training for, etc., is huge relative to the average boring webinar.

SIX TIPS FOR WORKING WITH YOUR PRODUCER

Ideally, the session producer is the one who pulls it all together (like the producer of a movie). In reality, it's often a person who can operate a piece of software, but may not have the project management and cat herding experience to help you rock. This is where you take responsibility for helping them help you.

1. Make sure you and the producer swap mobile phone numbers

If the world comes to an end, they need to know how to get ahold of you. For example, if their (or your) internet connection went down, would you be able to text or call? Perhaps even call into the audio conference and have the producer push the rest of your slides to finish the session?

2. Tell the producer how you'd adapt your presentation and interactions

I suggest starting with "You know how people do something like <this> in an in-person presentation? I want to do something like that in this event with you. How do we get creative to do something like that?" Alternatively, what I usually do is figure that out on my own and then tell the producer what I'm up to (there's a good chance they may not have seen it before).

3. Ask the producer what the parameters are for polling before sending them yours

Most polls are input into the software in advance. Some platforms have a limit to how long a question can be. They all have a limit to how many multiple choice answers there can be (and how long those can be, too. Some let you have "select all that apply" as an option. You don't have to be the expert on the software—you just have to ask better questions.

4. Be sure you know what link to join for the rehearsal

Some platforms will let you join the rehearsal using the exact same link that you'd use to join the actual event (and rehearse in that same "room"). Others may not. It's good to know.

5. Ask the producer if there are known issues with the software

There are no perfect platforms, and the person using it all the time will be the one in the know. Let the producer know what operating system you'll be using while you're at it—platforms often work a little differently on PC vs Mac (vs iPad/tablet).

6. Ask if there are other cool features to take advantage of

The potential number of options is big, but you never know when something cool bubbles up. One platform I know of will let you draw/annotate on a video. Several will integrate a Twitter stream. A few will let you plug in a different camera to use instead of your webcam. At least one will let you give attendees a button to screenshot your slide (nice for giving them another way to capture your contact details or a cool checklist to use right away). You get the idea.

The final thought

One darker note, and I only mean this in love. Producers want everything to go right (that's good!), but it often means they operate from a position of pain avoidance instead of a perspective of pursuing opportunity. Don't be entirely surprised if you hear "we don't do that," not because it *can't* be done, but because they're afraid. It's your show, and you're the leader. Now go lead.

SEVEN TIPS TO PASS ALONG TO YOUR INSTRUCTIONAL DESIGNER

Instructional design (ID) is a specialized discipline that connects the dots between organizational goals, performance improvement, curriculum design, and measurable outcomes. As mentioned earlier, however, there's a huge emphasis on creating on-demand/e-learning content, so you may be guiding them to help you create rocking live classes that are more than talking-over-slides. Here are some ideas.

1. Help your ID understand the nuance of live, virtual delivery

Think about how written music works. Looking at something on a piece of paper is a FAR cry from real music, right? So what do composers and arrangers do? They include a myriad of annotations that give a musician looking at the sheet music direction on volume and tempo and repeats and mood and on and on. And instructional designers should take note (pun fully intended).

2. Start with the affective (emotional) first

Given that we've two important sides to the brain and a lot of training content is one-sided, I'd start with adding in ideas for improving affective impact. Example: perhaps one point in the content is about the dire consequences of a mistake that is to be avoided. Saying a few words is one thing. It's another to:

- allow time for the learners to reflect on or personalize that impact.

- ask for learners to generate their own answers instead of giving them one.
- deepen that reflection by spending the time to ask more questions. "Why is that important?" "Tell me more?" "Who else would be impacted and how?"

3. Add in notes about pace, pause, and phrasing

Speakers, storytellers, and musicians all use variance as a means of getting and keeping attention and improving retention. Not every slide or exercise has to have the same duration. What if one part of a slide deck had a series of visuals that went by quickly as part of a story? Then perhaps you pause for an interaction for application, discussion, reflection? Again, you're making it up, but a few notes go a long way.

4. Leave room for the "performer" (that's you!) to interpret

It's possible to overdo it. There's no magic way to figure this out . . . it might be that you do or don't know the facilitator(s) who will be delivering your stuff, it might be an adjustment or suggestion based on culture, and on and on. Keeping with the other performance analogies, though, actors and musicians both take cues from scripts, directors, and sheet music, and bring something of their own to the table. Great trainers and facilitators will do the same. Ones that aren't so great, well, won't. Different problem to solve.

5. Move some content to other media

Live human interactions are a huge part of learning, and virtual classrooms a great medium for concurrent collaboration. Shorten the amount of time you talk by making some content available elsewhere.

6. **Plan to demonstrate interaction almost immediately in the live session**

It's likely your learners have experienced webinars that were "listen and watch" experiences, and they'll likely bring the presupposition to your class that "this is one of those." Get to "do and share" quickly.

7. **Tell 'em to help you find your inner Elvis**

IDs are a creative bunch. Encourage them to be creative. Do you break into a different voice or character? Get loud to emphasize something? Assuming it's consistent with your style of delivery, turn the ID into a partner for coming up with new and fun ways to make the virtual classroom experience something fun.

The final thought

There's a huge opportunity in the world of learning and development to positively impact people's lives. Add to this that an awesome and engaged facilitator (again, that's you!) and you'll add a multiplier effect that leaves learners equipped and motivated to go conquer the world.

FOUR IDEAS TO IMPROVE YOUR WEBINAR INTRODUCTION

A moderator sharing something about you is typically a participant's first impression of you. Here's how to make it better.

1. Get clear on your bio's purpose

The word "bio" (biography) is a misnomer. Audiences really don't care that you won an award in sixth grade for rescuing a unicorn. Bios serve one function: to motivate attention and involvement. They're more an introduction than a biography. Answer the audience's Big Implicit Question: Do you have credibility? In their unspoken words, *"Should I listen, and trust that you can deliver on what's been promised?"*

2. Approach the biography as supporting evidence for THIS session

Take a hatchet to every detail that is even close to marginally irrelevant to the audience. Don't think, "Super-duper short." Think, "Super-duper relevant details for THIS webinar or virtual class." Include as much as needed to answer the Big Implicit Question. No less. No more.

3. Don't be afraid of humor—especially with humorless audiences

Supporting evidence doesn't have to be limited to your alma mater. And in some industries that have been especially scrubbed within an inch of their lives, there's a huge opportunity to be a welcome face in a sea of boring. People relate to people. My bet is that you're pretty interesting during Happy Hour. Tap in to the (suitable for work) elements of your interestingness.

4. Write your bio as a performance to be read aloud

Even a great bio is dead in the water if it fails to get attention and incite anticipation. Which means that how it's delivered could actually hurt the cause. Remember, the brain avoids boring. Great performance itself is a compelling thing to listen to. Avoid complex sentences, and write in an active voice.

The final thought

Presentations and classes have a flow to them, a rhythm. If and when you work with someone who will introduce you, the momentum has the potential to go beyond words. It sets the stage for your entrance. Own it!

SIX WAYS TO HELP YOUR MODERATOR HELP YOU ROCK

Webinar moderators come in all shapes and sizes. A few are former radio pros who kick real butt. More commonly they're an extra person in the company, an editor from the publication where you rented the list, or (gasp) a senior executive who nobody can say no to.

1. Don't be shy about asking the moderator to practice

An introduction that "sounds like it's being read" is a lot less energetic and compelling than something that sounds conversational. You win when the moderator wins.

2. Make sure they know how to pronounce difficult names, particularly yours

Don't make assumptions here, because the potential impact for you is down the road. Will that person who refers you down the road or calls you to follow up know how to pronounce your name? That will be more comfortable for them when they're "in the know."

3. Consider letting the moderator re-write or edit your bio

Just because you wrote your intro to be read doesn't mean that it's comfortable to read for someone else. Know what your own negotiables and non-negotiables are. And if you say yes to letting them alter your bio—ask to see the final product (duh).

4. Tell the moderator how to interject with questions

Note the assumption here that I'm presuming you're evolving past "45 minutes plus Q&A at the end." I tell 'em just to call out my name like, *"Hey Roger!"* Then when I finish a sentence or find a natural place to pause I say, *"Yeah James, whatcha got?"*

5. Tell the moderator what questions to look for and which to avoid

If you're lucky, you'll have more questions submitted than you have time for. Give the moderator an idea of the kinds of questions you'd love to answer and those you'd love to avoid. Impact goes up. Discomfort goes down.

6. Invite the moderator to play "color commentator"

This is admittedly an advanced idea, because it's beyond the skill of many moderators. Done well, however, the moderator can interject comments from the audience such as, *"Hey Roger, Juli makes a good add-on point to what you just said . . ."*

The final thought

Audience is investing heavily of their time to be with you, and perhaps more importantly, your personal brand is on the line at a time when all eyes are watching. The potential benefit a professional moderator brings to you cannot be overstated.

SEVEN IDEAS FOR YOUR
OPENING AND CLOSING SLIDES

The typical webinar has an introduction and a closing that involves a moderator welcoming participants, covering a couple housekeeping items, reminding them of next steps, etc. This list is for those things that you as the presenter can influence in their (the moderator's) content to better set yourself up for success.

1. Use a visual to let participants know how to submit questions

Don't just *say*, also *show* a screenshot. You'll better cater to varying learning preferences, and some late arrivers may be present on the web conference without an audio connection.

2. Remind participants how to hear the session

How to connect aurally is part of every platform's invitation copy, but people often don't read it. If they're logged in but not connected to the audio yet, a visual reminder will help 'em get there.

3. Promote a future event

You've got a captive audience. There's no better time, assuming the future event is relevant to them, to add value by sharing a future event notification as an additional resource for them.

4. Remind participants to fill out the exit survey and when it will appear

You never get 100% participation in an exit survey, but it doesn't hurt to ask explicitly. Bonus: it's not uncommon for participants to ask how to do it. Know how it works (e.g., "upon exiting the webinar" or whatever is true for you).

5. Share the session's Twitter hashtag

Even if you hate Twitter, it's useful to later go look at what participants found relevant enough to share with their followers. Go to the URL search.twitter.com to search on the session's hashtag and start analyzing.

6. Show a picture of your book or other resource

People rarely want to be sold, but mentioning that you have a book or paper or other resource can both build credibility and be done in the context of being helpful.

7. Tell 'em how to connect with you after the session

I'm not a big fan of using slide decks as handouts, but many people do. Sharing how to find you on LinkedIn (or equivalent) will help you build your tribe. Inviting further questions may seem like extra work, but it's huge for engagement and your personal brand.

The final thought

You may not be delivering the opening and closing sequences of the session, but treat it as if your personal brand is on the line. The worst thing that happens is that you help someone else grow, and that's a valuable deposit in your account of social capital.

CHAPTER 4

Going Live

SIX IDEAS FOR CONQUERING
ANXIETY ABOUT VIRTUAL SESSIONS

You've spent all your life talking with people in the same room. You haven't put in the same time delivering virtual presentations or classes. Feeling a bit of apprehension is natural. Here are a few things my coaching clients have found useful.

1. Remember that authenticity trumps perfection every time

This is *especially* true online. The bar is low—there are so many talk-AT-you webinars in the world that your talk-WITH-you delivery will rock their world.

2. Learn only what you need to know about the platform

The goal isn't "how to use software," it's "communicate effectively." Start with learning only what you need to succeed with the next session. *Then* add something new.

3. Get help

A moderator or co-facilitator will give you a feeling of support. A good one will take some tasks off your plate. A great one follows your lead; doesn't disrupt your momentum, becomes the voice of the audience; gives you a sense of the audience's presence and thoughts.

4. Have a backup plan

Don't drive yourself mad what-iffing yourself to death. Your plan might be as simple as rescheduling the session. Just making a list of a few scenarios and what you'll do is salve to the raging soul (i.e., "if my VoIP audio connection cuts out, I'll have the phone number to the telephone audio conference written down so I can dial back in quickly).

5. Remember that things go wrong with in-person presentations; too

People are late because of a car accident, projector bulbs go out, or a fire alarm that evacuates the building and wastes 30 minutes. You don't call it a failure; you adjust.

6. Let creativity rule

I've seen people put up a picture of an audience on the wall in front of them, post a little mirror on the side of their monitor, even take Valium. Anxiety in some form is normal, and the remedy is usually quite personal.

The final thought

I'm no psychologist, and the list herein could go on and on. I'm not a big fan of *eradication* so much as conquering through *adaptation*. To be sure, nothing beats enough practice or repetition so your basic actions are more autonomic, but I'm pretty sure nobody's ever died from a botched virtual presentation or class. That's at least a little bit of comfort, right?

SIX WAYS TO SOUND AND FEEL MORE ENERGETIC

An old adage when training telephone-based customer service reps is, "Let them hear you smile." When you move a presentation or class online, it's common to feel a change of energy in the new environment, especially before you get used to using your platform's dashboard to "see" your participants. Here are some quick ideas to help you bring authenticity and energy to your virtual gig.

1. Become aware of (and adjust for) the bio-feedback you're receiving

We adjust our energy, in part, from how we hear ourselves. It's usually unconsciously. Two big contributors are 1) a headset that either blocks some of our environment sound or feeds it back into our ear directly and/or 2) the fact that we're in a (usually) smaller space environmentally.

2. Find a new physical space

Even if the new physical space is about the same size and sound as the previous one, a change of physical space puts us in a new head space.

3. Stand up

Remember, when you present in-person you're almost always standing. Don't underestimate how much sitting down changes that energy and tonality.

4. Pick up the pace a bit

Remember, participants are having a psychosocial experience that's closer to watching television than being at an in-person seminar. They're used to a pace that keeps things moving.

5. Listen to a recording of yourself

The closest thing you can get to hearing yourself objectively is to listen while you're not speaking. Here's one place where the ease of pushing a "record" button in your web conferencing solution is worth even more money. Bonus: do five or ten minutes of your material during a rehearsal to get more return on that time invested.

6. Get a tough-but-loving coach

Most people hate the way they sound (it's natural—you're used to hearing yourself through the bones in your head). Better: give someone else permission to give you candid feedback. Best: make sure that someone else has experience with vocal training *in a media environment* (e.g., voice-overs, radio, webinars, etc.).

The final thought

You might not be a professional speaker, but you are a professional who speaks. Remember that your audience will likely never consciously notice how you are "different from those other people," but the energy you deliver—even to a remote audience—will set you apart.

SIX TIPS FOR HELPING YOUR VOICE SOUND AWESOME

In two different studies I've done, survey respondents have rated the use of voice as more important in a virtual presentation or class than for an in-person equivalent. It makes sense—the sensory inputs of a virtual participant are proportioned differently (especially if you're not appearing on webcam). Here are some easy ideas anyone can use.

1. Open up your "core"

Your core is roughly the part of you between your neck and legs. The problem is that most virtual presentations are made sitting down, and this makes it harder to take full, diaphragmatic breaths that support good vocal tone.

2. Speak from your lower middle voice

You can't change the voice you were born with, but you *can* change how well you use it. Your own optimum resonance is found in your lower middle voice. To find it, purse your lips and make an mmmmm sound from the top of your range to the bottom, finding the lower middle part of that range.

3. (Additionally) create meaning with inflection

Remember, your voice is carrying more of the meaning-making. What may sound a little over-the-top to you doesn't to your audience. I promise.

4. Place your headset microphone close to your face to improve resonance

A microphone's "proximity effect" is how it picks up lower frequencies, and this decreases dramatically as the microphone is farther away from the sound source (your mouth). Having the mic close to your mouth will *dramatically* improve how well you sound.

5. Place your headset microphone below your lips to eliminate pops

A risk of a proximate microphone is that it picks up the pops of your speech (such as words using the letter p). Position it just below your lips to avoid 'em.

6. Skip the speakerphone or area mic

Any microphone designed to pick up a non-direct signal (including the one on your laptop) will pick up ambient noise, but there's a more insidious villain lurking, too: hearing your room's space. It's called reverberation. It makes you sound weird, and it makes recordings sound even weirder.

The final thought

Your actual, real, sound-making voice is a signature. It's uniquely you. And it's even more important when your participants are in this new sensory environment. Pay attention to it and it'll pay dividends.

NINE IDEAS FOR USING YOUR WEBCAM MORE EFFECTIVELY

Should you use your webcam? The empirical research is sparse and undecided, but I've asked the question of thousands (literally) of webinar attendees. Their preference is clear—use it. We do know from science that people tend to connect with others' faces, and I think that used well, appearing on webcam is a powerful engagement tool. Here are some ideas for making the most of it.

1. Eliminate environmental and background distractions

Participants don't expect you to have a composed environment like a broadcast network. That whiteboard with writing all over it? That open window with people walking by outside? Different story.

2. Adjust expressions and body language for the camera's eye

A webcam is a near-field camera, meaning it's designed to be optimum when you're 18-30 inches away. It also means that it'll accentuate your facial expressions. And if you want body language to have an impact, make sure that it doesn't extend outside the camera's field of vision.

3. Position yourself back from the camera but within reach of your keyboard

Getting back from the camera will help minimize how it accentuates your facial expressions, but you still need to operate the computer if you want to maximize the use of tools and engagement. Make sure you can reach without stretching or changing your body position.

4. Balance the lighting on your face

Photographers use a three-point lighting system—two in front of you and one behind. While a good option, it also may not be practical. Your goal should be to not only make sure you can be seen, but also to eliminate shadows under your eyes, behind your eyeglasses, or other situation that minimizes the impact of your awesome visage.

5. Know what participants are seeing

You can test this yourself, but it's better to have someone else's (more objective) opinion. Have them look at your lighting, background, and especially any objects that are particularly distracting. Power tip: make sure you don't have a line (like the bottom of a whiteboard) that intersects with (looks like it's coming out of) your head.

6. Make eye contact definitively

Eye contact when using a webcam is particularly unnatural, but the opportunity is profound. Think about when a newscaster looks directly into the camera—it looks like they're making direct eye contact with you. Bonus: you don't have to sustain it 100% of the time, but be purposeful about this eye contact during your opening, closing, and for any key points.

7. Be aware of behavioral distractions

Even if no one's ever said anything to you about your in-person behaviors, remember that the webcam is going to show you differently. Better: consider asking a friend to privately chat you if there's something distracting that you keep doing. Best: address it *before* a session, not during.

8. Hold a physical object close to your face

I learned this from Pat Dooris, a veteran television reporter in the Portland, Oregon market. You want to make sure that something you hold the audience to see is, in fact, seen (like your book). It feels unnatural to hold it close to your face, but it'll make sure it's seen on camera.

9. Tell participants to look at the camera

It's best to keeping "calling back" participants' attention in any context, but if you're going to demonstrate something via webcam, explicitly tell 'em to look.

The final thought

The research is still sparse on using webcam video, but anecdotally I've asked thousands of people (during webinars) if they prefer seeing someone on camera. The answer is an overwhelming, "yes!"

A few years back I did a global survey of nearly 1200 people. The whole paper, including the research results are in the extras section (www.thevirtualpresenter.com/playbookextras).

THIRTEEN IDEAS FOR YOUR "GO LIVE" CHECKLIST

Typical meetings don't require you to show up early. A virtual presentation or class, however, isn't a typical meeting. Being purposeful about your approach—the process by which you get ready mentally, physically, and technically—will be highly individualized for you, but turning it into a checklist so that you don't forget something is strongly suggested. Here are few ideas.

1. Log in fifteen minutes before anyone else

Joining the "green room" 30 minutes early is a typical practice, but your goal isn't to be typical (I hope). The worst that happens is that you're waiting on others and you get a moment to check Facebook one more time.

2. Ensure web and audio connectivity success

Ideally you'll be using the exact same setup as during rehearsal, but you can't be too careful. Use speedtest.net (or the equivalent) to make sure your bandwidth is appropriate, and *the most important thing to test is upload, not download, speed.* Even if you don't know what "appropriate" is, how does it compare to normal?

3. Hang a *Do Not Disturb—Webinar in Progress* sign on the door

Even if someone knocks, your attention will be diverted. And some people knock anyway (they think it's an emergency). Tell 'em (on the sign) it's because you're doing a virtual session and they'll also realize that they should keep the noise down.

4. Send a final copy of your slides to the moderator or team

Even if your connection to the interwebs takes a dump, they can pull up your slides and help you continue.

5. Print your final slides or notes

In the event of web failure, if you've got your notes, you can continue—assuming you know how to direct others to advance your slides.

6. Jot down the audio conference number (and PIN!) on your notes printout

A down web connection means your VoIP will be offline, too. Dialing back in with your mobile is easy, but that's not when you want to go looking for the number in the email application you've closed.

7. Reboot your computer

Never assume your computer is fine because it hasn't had issues during the hours it's been on. I'll spare you the technical baloney. Just do it.

8. Close all unnecessary apps

Some auto-start during startup, others you may have opened to get ready for your session. Free up all the horsepower your computer can muster, which means minimize the number of places it's using it.

9. Turn off notifications and background processes

Do you auto-sync to the cloud? See email notifications? Have a backup program that runs every hour? Auto-install operating system or software-as-a-service application updates? Turn 'em off.

10. Get a glass of water that's room temperature

Cold water might be refreshing, but it'll constrict your vocal cords. Better: have a whole bottle of water (you may use more than you think).

11. Take a hiatus from caffeine

You may not notice the effect caffeine has on you because you're a regular user, but it will exacerbate any anxiety you have (even if you don't think you're anxious). Tension's not good, especially in the "take full breaths and sound awesome" department.

12. Review session logistics with the team

You covered 'em in rehearsal because you're a pro, but don't assume people remember. How will the session start? Who's pushing the record button and when? Does the moderator and/or behind-the-scenes team know how to handle questions? How are transitions being handled between speakers? How does the session end? Will there be a post-session debrief and if so, what URL/conference login is needed?

13. Take a moment to meditate or center yourself

Visualize what is important for you. For example, when you deliver someone an idea that will change their life, what will the expression on their face be? It's still going to happen, because you're awesome—just figure out how to be present with that when they're not sitting right in the same room as you.

The final thought

The second most important thing here isn't to get overwhelmed with a lengthy list, which is why turning these things into a checklist is valuable. The most important? Personalize the list (e.g., what does centering yourself look like?) and the order in which they fall for you (e.g., you may find that getting water while your computer reboots is what works for you). What separates pros from amateurs isn't the live gig itself, it's the preparation. Now, go rock it.

FIVE IDEAS FOR AFTER YOUR SESSION

Often what feels weird about online presentations or classes isn't something we even notice: we miss the social interaction that happens afterwards. This isn't exhaustive by any means, but here are a few things that have worked well for me.

1. Block out your calendar for the time immediately following your session

You can't "hang out in the hallway" if you don't have the time. Relationship-building pays long-term dividends, and just because you're online doesn't mean it can't happen.

2. Personally send a note to all who tweeted or commented

Whoah! Sounds like a lot of work, right? Yup. But no one ever built a following, tribe, or bus full of groupies because they just disappeared. For me it's usually Twitter, and I say, "Thanks for being there. It's an honor to have had your attention, and thanks for tweeting!" Or something like that.

3. "Favorite" or capture the nice comments made in public

If you go to www.thevirtualpresenter.com, you'll see I have both traditional testimonials and "tweetimonials." These are but a portion of the hundreds of nice comments I've seen after events, about one of my books, etc. Like somebody writing about you in the New York Times, these are public. Cite them appropriately and they make a nice addition to your curriculum vitae.

4. Ask for LinkedIn references

I confess I'm lousy at this, but right after a presentation (where your audience is, by definition, already sitting at their computer) is a smokin' hot time to get them to take action.

5. Answer their questions via email, blog, or both

I invite people to contact me. It takes extra time, but here's why it's worth it. One, it almost always has their email signature. Two, I get to be of service. Three, sometimes I answer their question and then ask for a testimonial. Four, sometimes I (anonymously) use their question to prompt a blog post. Win, win, win, win.

The final thought

You have your own motivations for what you do, but in today's world, you increasingly need to build your own brand, *even if* you have a day job and intend to keep it. There's nothing that endears you to an employer like having a fan base that vouches for the "soft" value you contribute to the organization (and not everything you do shows up in a quarterly report, right?). Relationship is the oldest new killer app.

CHAPTER 5

Overlooked
Tactics and Tools

THIRTY-EIGHT OVERLOOKED NUGGETS ABOUT PLATFORM FEATURES (AND GETTING THE MOST FROM THEM)

Even after sixteen years in the web conferencing industry, I see really cool features go under- or unutilized. This chapter's dedicated to helping you avoid mistakes and avoid missing out on the opportunity to maximize your web conferencing investment. Bear in mind that it's not exhaustive (you wouldn't really read a 400-page book about web conferencing software), it's just the "wish I'd known this back then" stuff.

Audio

1. Consider a toll-free number when your market warrants it

It's less important now than when people paid hefty long distance bills, and most people in the corporate world stopped worrying about long distance costs a long time ago. There are still, however, market segments where a toll-free number is invaluable, and some vendors give you the option of having one (especially for international markets).

2. Use a USB headset as your first choice

For most people, the best way to sound good is with a USB headset. First, with a professional web conferencing platform, USB audio sounds better than the telephone. Second, it stays a consistent distance from your mouth. Three, unlike speakerphones, it doesn't pick up ambient environmental noise. You'll sound better and have less to worry about.

3. (Almost always) give attendees the option of telephone or computer audio

In today's access-your-session-from-any-device world, you want to make it easy, and options are good. When would you not provide the option? When you know exactly what their attendance environment is or when you want to force them into one way of joining the audio conference (yes, there are times and reasons to do that).

Webcam and presenter video

4. Change the aspect ratio of your webcam to capture more body language

"Aspect ratio" is the ratio of width to length. PowerPoint, for instance, was 4:3 for a long time, but now is "widescreen" or 16:9. Some platforms give you the choice to switch to 16:9, too—useful if you are expressive with your upper extremities.

5. Use a camera other than your webcam

Plugging in a separate camera gives you a number of options. It's useful when you want to have two people sit at a desk (like a television studio) or show a whole panel of speakers who are in one room. You might also use it when you have a roomful of participants—you've a lot more flexibility to position it to see the room than simply turning a computer around to use the webcam.

Screen sharing

6. "Change presenters" to let someone else share from their desktop

This is more powerful than going through all that pre-production to try to get different presenters' content into one slide deck. And if one of those presenters wants to show something else from their desktop, they can.

7. Pause your screen sharing to navigate privately

Maybe you want to navigate to a folder that you don't want the audience to see, but probably the most powerful use of pausing one's screen is that you can skip ahead or back in your PowerPoint presentation without making anyone dizzy wondering what you're doing.

8. Share keyboard and mouse control

Give another presenter the ability to control your keyboard and mouse, and they can navigate your computer as if they were sitting at it. This is most useful when you are collaborating on a single document (e.g., showing one PowerPoint deck but want each presenter to be able to navigate their portion of the presentation).

Visuals and non-webcam video

9. Check the resolution of your screen sharing

Some platforms default to a screen sharing resolution that is less than full color. This isn't a big deal if you don't care how your slides look, or you could be like me and it drives you nuts. Note two things: your platform may not have settings to adjust because it's always full color, and two, for those that do adjust, that may be at the individual session level or at the global/account level.

10. Give yourself time for your slides to upload

The benefit of slides "uploading to the system" is that once they're uploaded (read: converted), there'll be less latency (delay) for your participants (less an issue now than in yesteryear). The downside? Conversion takes time, and you'll want to triple check that your graphics and colors rendered correctly (sometimes they don't).

11. Show a video that's embedded natively, not from your desktop

You can show the audience anything that's on your computer screen, but your computer's only going to recognize one audio source (your telephone or USB headset). In other words, your audience won't hear it. Different platforms have different ways of handling this (e.g., upload a video file, switch to a video file, or play from a URL such as YouTube), but use their 'native' way of doing it.

12. Pay attention to your "audience view" when showing video

I'll spare you the technical details, but you'll want to know what your audience is seeing. Some platforms' way of showing video might result in participants' viewing of said video in a way that ends at slightly different times, and you'll want to know when it's time to keep moving.

13. Share an in-room whiteboard or flipchart

This is a rare feature for virtual presentation solutions, but some will auto-sense the corners of a whiteboard or flipchart and "square it up" in participants' viewing area. The benefit is that you can do your thing at the whiteboard and participants will have a clear view of what you're writing or drawing.

Recordings and screenshots

14. Choose where you want your recordings to go

Some platforms give you the choice of changing the default folder where a recording is placed, once made. It's less of an issue if all you're going to do is upload it to the platform's hosting solution (or not at all if you can only record to the cloud), but *really* useful if you want to save the recording file for editing or use elsewhere because you won't be worrying about how to move a 50 or 500 megabyte file.

15. Let participants make their own recordings

When participants love you and share what you do, letting them make their own recording is useful. I've used this in virtual classes where they want to be able to fairly instantly review discussions that weren't part of the slides or workbook.

16. Instruct participants how to take their own screenshots

Many people don't know how to do this on their computer, let alone in the web conferencing platform. Some platforms give your participants a button to instantly take a snapshot of something they see that they'd like to save for later.

Scheduling and course catalogs

17. Copy a previous session setup to save time when scheduling a new one

Platforms are smart enough to know that you want the new session at a new date and time. You'll save the time you spent getting colors and images right. NOTE: if you've customized the confirmation, reminder, and follow up emails (I do suggest you do!), you may want to double check that they still say what you want.

18. Create a single landing page that hosts multiple different sessions

The value here is simple and powerful: your invitation brings an invitee to a single URL. They can pick and choose multiple sessions to register for, but only have to register one time.

19. Create a single registration page for an event series or sequence

Engagement *over time* is powerful for marketers, and can you imagine a group of students wanting to register separately for the six sessions you'll host in a six-week class? Earn bonus points if you want to make participation in the second or subsequent session contingent on having been at the previous session (and your platform supports it).

20. Use on-the-fly (instant) sessions to improve communication over a simple phone call

When you like seeing someone's face and getting real, collaborative work done, you get addicted to web and video conferencing. It won't be the default for many people in your life, though. When they call you, use an instant meeting to up the value of the time spent. Bonus: do this with a "webinar" for crisis communications or getting the word out quickly to your team.

21. Start an on-the-fly session from inside an application

This is admittedly more a collaboration feature than one you'll use in a virtual presentation or class, but I assume you'll use web conferencing for more than one use case. Imagine firing up a video/web/audio conference from inside instant messaging or a document you're working on. Powerful.

Participant registration and entry

22. Change your platform's default color scheme to create a new feeling

Your organization likely put a lot of thought into the "color palette" it uses. It's part of what is subconsciously communicated in everything it touches. Add your web conferencing platform to the mix.

23. Use an "eye dropper" or "color picker" to determine the hex code of a color in an image

Okay, this isn't a web conferencing feature, but it's useful when combined with the ability to change your platform's color scheme. Determining a color's hex (hexadecimal) code (unique identifier) is easy with the right tool. Such a tool may be built into your operating system, an application, or you can easily find a free one by search the web for "get colors from image."

24. Remember that "put your logo here" doesn't have to be a logo

You're uploading an image file (e.g., .jpg). It can be anything you want. Get creative and you can promote your next event, share a social media URL, or a number of other things.

25. Use "approve/deny" to be selective about who can attend

"Approve/deny" is a feature that adds your ability to choose whether or not someone can attend your session. Chronologically it's a step in between two things: someone registering for your session and them getting the email confirmation with the details about how to join your session.

26. Avoid using "approve/deny" if you want to let in last-minute registrants

The last thing you want to be doing five minutes before a session is fielding notifications that someone else wants to attend.

27. Use a "waiting room" to host participants before you go live

Think of this like a virtual foyer. Participants benefit because the system lets them "into the hallway but not into the hall" and they know they're in the right place.

28. Customize your waiting room to prompt other activity

While participants are waiting for the session to start, they *could* have further instructions. Examples might include joining on Twitter with the appropriate hashtag, downloading a participant guide or worksheet, or sending in an early question.

29. Limit class sizes when you need to manage specific exercises

In an in-person setting, some forms of training, coaching, and interaction need to happen in rooms with a limited number of participants. Very few web conferencing platforms let you *limit* class sizes, but the same dynamic you experience offline translates online. Bonus points if your platform will automatically open a seat back up if a full class has someone drop out.

Presenters and presenting

30. Assign technical or access privileges based on a presenter's responsibilities

Some platforms allow you to give differing levels of control to presenters. Some roles limit access to the platform's features (e.g., no ability to start/stop the recording, shut down the session, etc.), which is useful for guests, panelists, or people who don't think before pushing buttons.

31. Use a virtual "green room" to center the presentation team before going live

The "green room" or holding area separate from the live stage, has many uses in the virtual world. It's a powerful function for presenters who are in different places to be able to talk, review the session's flow, etc., before being live in front of an audience.

32. Use private chat like whispering to the person next to you

Whether or not you open up chat for all participants, familiarize the presentation team with how to chat with each other. "Speak louder" or "You've got five minutes to go" or a hundred other things that don't need to be shared in front of the whole audience.

33. Share a hot link in chat or questions

When presenting, you'll probably not be typing responses back to people who have submitted questions textually, but the same feature can be used to share a link to the whole audience. One of my faves: I just showed you a website, and now I copy the URL and paste it out for all to click on. Bonus: better platforms make this a "hot" link, meaning it's clickable (versus a participant having to copy/paste it).

34. Practice in the same "room" that you'll be in for the live session

When you speak at an in-person function, it's useful to walk the room in advance, right? (Yes, it is.) Online, some platforms let you practice in the exact "room" you'll be in. This means that setting up polls or saving your desktop configuration are things you can do without the time pressure of "going live" in a few minutes.

Breakout rooms

35. Decide if breakout groups will be random, manual, or self-selected

Breaking a large group into smaller groups for hands-on work is a common training or facilitator tactic, but most web conferencing platforms do *not* support this. When you use breakouts, figure out (in advance, presumably) *how* you want participants to work with each other.

36. Make sure groups know how to get your attention

When in a breakout group, does a participant simply need to raise their hand? Can they use private chat to you?

37. Set a timer to keep things moving

Some platforms have built-in timers so small groups know how much time they have. Using such is better than asking people to keep an eye on a clock, because you have control and the experience is the same for all groups.

38. "Walk around the room" to visit each group

This is what you do in an in-person session, right? (Yes, you do.) There's nothing quite like listening in on small groups doing work to let you know if they understand and are making progress. Just like in-person groups, there's always "that one group," right? (Yes, there is.)

The final thought

Perhaps one of the most important things to remember, as I've noted elsewhere in this book, the potential list of things to do is long. There's no substitute for just diving in and figuring it out, but the best long-term strategy is to grow a little at a time. Pick up something here and there, and use this book as a reference.

And remember: there's no perfect "right" way, even for a guy who's done this 1000 times more than you. Be of good cheer. You will be a rock star in your virtual "room" before you know it.

TEN THINGS I LIKE ABOUT CITRIX GOTOMEETING, GOTOWEBINAR, AND GOTOTRAINING

When we present, train, or facilitate in an in-person room, we understand that several dynamics affect how we connect with the audience. These often include how many delegates are present, how we intend to interact with them or have them interact with each other, and how the seating is arranged.

These same factors are present when you host sessions online, too. It is also why forward-thinking vendors like Citrix have different configurations of their web conferencing software. Like an in-person room, there is no one-size-fits-all approach.

What follows are my unvarnished, independent opinions as a user, analyst, and old-timer in the web conferencing industry. The foundation of all of them is this: value is created in ways that most people don't see upon first glance.

Here's to making you smarter and wiser than those who don't see.

1. GoToMeet.me—your persistent, branded URL

GoToMeet.me—your persistent, branded URL

GoToMeet.me is a brand new service for all licensed GoToX users. In short, it's a customizable URL (mine is www.gotomeet.me/RogerCourville)

that serves as a consistent place to launch GoToMeeting. And it's perhaps the most overlooked value going. Here's why:

Imagine how often you'd use the telephone if you had to *schedule* your use of it. True enough, most "meetings" are something you put on the calendar sometime in the future, but if you'll transform your paradigm of web conferencing to more like how you use the telephone, you'll see a spike in productivity in several ways (as examples):

- You'll save the time of scheduling individual meetings (e.g., coaching sessions, contract talks, etc.) in GoToMeeting.
- An incoming phone call can be instantly turned into a web/video conference to get work done now instead of scheduling (and potentially rescheduling) in the future.
- Your clients will get used to the same URL and, assuming they know your name, aren't trying to remember a meeting name such as 2189Mks4. (I append mine to my email signature.)
- The associated phone number is persistent (read: easy for you to remember), so it's easy to include phone-only participants on the fly.

In addition to the productivity gains, you can change the look/feel of your gotomeet.me landing page with your picture, colors of choice, and a link you can direct anywhere you want (mine goes to my LinkedIn profile).

2. Sightboard makes your physical whiteboard virtual

Sightboard's a new feature available in all three products that smartly senses the corners of a whiteboard or flipchart *in the physical room* and displays it for virtual participants. Better yet, even if the whiteboard is at an angle, Sightboard "squares it up" so participants see it like they would a PowerPoint slide you're showing. This radically transforms your work in two critical ways.

One, you're liberated from your desktop visually. You've long been able to use more than PowerPoint (via screen sharing). If you wanted to draw on the fly, however, your input tools were your mouse or trackpad for whatever application you were drawing with. Now if you're more comfortable with a "real" whiteboard (most of us are), use it along with your other options.

Two, you now easily bridge the in-person room and the online participants. Unless you present or train only one way (e.g., all keynote speeches from the front of the room), the question isn't *if* you'll face the need to do this, it is *when* you'll need to accommodate participants in different spaces.

3. Integrated telephone and VoIP is a must-have for smooth audio interactions (and saving money)

Get your head out of the "webinars are talk-at-you" realm and think about what we do in-person. Unless you're doing all the talking in a session (and most of the time you shouldn't), speaking in a fluid manner is a *critical* part of being natural and engaged. Compare that with what happens online. The biggest barrier to natural speech is that it's not natural for participants to do so.

Making interaction a lot more natural comes down to control—whose audio line is open, whose is muted, and *most* importantly, your ability to either mute/unmute people on-the-fly or let them mute/unmute themselves.

I'll spare you the techie stuff. Trust me that you want to 1) be able to give participants a choice of audio options; 2) have it be easy to control. Engagement will go through the roof, and you'll get those "you're not like other webinars" comments.

Here's a bonus: when audio conferencing is built into the platform (with direct-dial numbers for more countries than you'll ever need), you'll not need to spend another dime on audio conferencing or look unprofessional by using free-conference-calling-and-a-donut-too service.

4. Undock your control panels to customize your presenter view

This is so important that I wrote a long blog post about it (see it here http://bit.ly/1TIasbc). Citrix's ability to "undock" (move) the panels (e.g., questions or polls) is my single favorite feature of their whole solution. Here's why:

The single biggest complaint about presenting/training online is, "I can't see my audience." True. *But that doesn't mean you're blind.*

The answer is re-arranging the Citrix tools so you can, *at a glance*, see activity that gives you insight about what people are doing. There are more than I'll list here (I'll treat the attention meter separately), but if you do nothing else, figure out which tools you're going to use *and re-arrange them so you can use them on-the-fly*. Again, read that blog post.

5. Use the attention meters to hone your talk

The attention meter is another tool (GoToWebinar and GoToTraining only) for keeping an eye on your audience that's worth a special mention. Unlike Questions or Chat, the Attention Meter keeps you abreast of passivity.

The attention meter basically detects the active window on a participant's desktop. In smaller sessions you could actually see who that is by individual, but what I use is the part that notes what percentage of the audience is "with me." (By the way, don't expect it to be 100%...it's not when you're in-person, and don't expect it offline, either).

So how do you use it? The same way you keep an eye on attention when in person. What happens when you see attention wane? You mix it up. Online you can ask a question, use a poll, take a break, call on the person in question, or whatever. Powerful.

Here's a bonus: the 'attention score' is also captured in reports. Want to evaluate what part of your session was more (or less) interesting? Want to know who was really paying attention? Bam!

6. Turn features on and off

The power of a conferencing solution isn't just in the existence of certain features . . . it's the ability to use them (or not) at the right time.

Example: I often use "hand up" as an indicator for seeing who in the audience wants to ask a live audio question (which I do by un-muting them, re-muting them after the question).

Here's the challenge: when you put your hand up online your arm doesn't get tired. Sometimes people "put up their hand" and leave it. Let's assume the best . . . sometimes people are just experimenting with stuff. Whatever the reason, when it comes to questions, I want to keep the seminar moving, and truth be told, I've called on someone with their hand up only to have them not be there.

Solution: depending on the event and situation, I often leave the "hand up" option off for the audience until I'm ready for audio questions. Then I know I'll get a live person . . . they just put up their hand! (Alternatively, there's an "all hands down" feature you can use to clear the cue).

One other note . . . this isn't the only feature that can be turned on/off in Citrix tools, it's just the example I've used. This ability to turn features on and off, however, is an important asset for anyone serious about impacting others with communication.

7. Use breakouts to facilitate individual/small group work

In-person sessions often have activities that involve something like "turn to the people at your table, work on <this>, and then we'll come back and talk about it as a group." And when was the last time you saw this in a webinar? Uh, never.

There are several reasons. One, most web conferencing vendors don't have breakout rooms. Two, it's mostly a training/facilitation use-case, and marketers of public webinars rarely think like trainers.

The science, however, is clear. Active participants learn more effectively than do passive participants.

In GoToTraining (only), you can break people into small groups either by assigning them or randomly. Then you as the presenter/facilitator can move from group to group (like you'd walk around to various tables in an in-person session).

8. Integrate PayPal for easy monetization

If you've ever set up a payment gateway with your bank, you know how many hours of messing around you will do. It's not for the faint of heart or wallet.

GoToTraining (only) integrates with a service anyone, anywhere can use (PayPal), but to me there's something more important than this—the fact that there are other parts of the training experience I want to customize.

For instance, when do I give them the .pdf of the workbook? In GoToTraining I can include a link in the confirmation email that they don't get until payment is confirmed.

Also, I already use PayPal to send out invoices, and for some clients I want to invoice them separately (so their participants don't have to use a credit card). This saves me time and gives me options.

9. Course catalog + reusable elements = less time and headache

This is a two-part favorite.

From an invitee's perspective, it's really useful to be able to come to a single registration page and see different classes at different times (or the same class offered at different times). Bonus: if a class is full, they see that, too and cannot register—more on that in a moment.

From my perspective, GoToTraining saves me a pile of time because I can duplicate classes (no need for entering the same data over and over), and I have a central library of resources that I can use for any/all classes (e.g., any multimedia file uploaded such as a video I'm going to show the class).

10. Limit class sizes to improve engagement (and monetization)

Typical webinars are "come one, come all," and that's not wrong. It's just not complete. Often for training or coaching, it's important to limit the size of the class.

This might be because you've planned activities based on how many people show up (e.g., you have five different "case studies" they'll work on in breakouts and don't want more than four people on a team so everyone is participative).

This also might be because you're charging for classes, and smaller classes with more engaged participants will yield better learning (and referrals). Or you know a client might be tempted to invite 500 people in the division (to save money), when they'd never do that if it was an in-person engagement.

The final thought

This editorial is "things I like." To be fair, it's worth commenting that I don't think there's any such thing as a perfect conferencing solution (just like there are features in Microsoft PowerPoint and Apple's Keynote that I wish I could combine into one perfect-for-me presentation software).

I realize that some of these are deeper-level features. But think about buying a car. It keeps you out of the rain, gets you to the store, and you don't even ask if it has an engine—but you begin to notice some of the distinguishing characteristics, the preferential little things that are really cool. Citrix solutions have many awesome features, and you're likely to find your favorite that isn't on my list.

That said, it's worth noting that one powerful aspect of Citrix's services is a fine balance of features and usability at a reasonable price. Said another way, it's not about software, it's about business value . . . something that should mean that the GoToMeeting, GoToWebinar, and/or GoToTraining should likely be on your short list to investigate.

Wait—one more!

11. *Look awesome* HD Faces video conferencing, even in low-bandwidth environments

Video is an important component of communication, but there's something special about the way Citrix approaches it. Besides an HD video experience, Citrix has cool behind-the-scenes technology that optimizes each participant's view based on their own web connectivity.

This is necessary, unfortunately, because each participant's local internet service provider is the least reliable part of the whole experience. Then, they often join with a wireless network, and wireless connections almost always have a performance cost. And the technology to make synchronous (real time) video work well is *radically* different than watching an on-demand video (like something on YouTube).

If I never brought it up, it's likely something you'd never notice. Just be aware that not all vendors' solutions are the same, and when you want to be a pro (not to mention have a lot less of that jumpy, pixelated video experience), it's useful to use professional tools.

EPILOGUE

"That! That right there! You can't DO that in a webinar!"

I was presenting a breakout session at a conference and I had just had participants do a small-group exercise at their table. Now this lady was getting "in my business" if you know what I mean. The room went silent waiting for me to respond.

Fortunately it was one of those times love prevailed. I softened my voice.

"You can't? Or you haven't seen it done?"

The number of features and options available in web conferencing platforms today is staggering. This is good or bad news. Good if you're going to dive in and want to do cool stuff. Bad if you think anyone (even someone like me) can keep abreast of 200+ vendors and their idiosyncrasies and you try to "know before you do."

It's also bad for you if you simply post something in a Facebook group asking, *"What's the best webinar platform?"* It might generate a few ideas for you, perhaps even some you like, but they're almost always sub-par relative to your interest in being a real pro.

There's a reason that the market leaders in webinar, webcast, and virtual classroom technologies are the leaders. There's a reason why they're not free. There's a reason why pro solutions are used by corporations and you may not be familiar with them as a solopreneur. And there's a reason why generic, public marketing webinars make use of so little of the power of web conferencing that you don't know what's possible and, at the same time, feel like the gal yelling at me.

No expert has all the answers, but they usually are better at asking the right questions. If I'm lucky at all with this book, it's that you have had both your mind expanded to possibilities and asking better questions, *and* you've realized that you can actually, really do this stuff. It's not hard, it's just different.

You will never, ever do all the things I've recommended here (and shouldn't even try) in a single session. You will, however, find that over time, perhaps with this tome as a reference, find different things that apply at different times, grow in your own ability to lead others who know less than you do, and drive real revenue or impact for your business or organization.

To your successes,
Roger

ACKNOWLEDGMENTS

Headshot

For the most amazing headshots ever, you have to check out AJ Coots at www.storytellingheadshots.com. There's a reason people actually fly to Portland (OR) just to have her shoot theirs (fortunately I live here).

Publishing

Maryanna Young and the crew at www.alohapublishing.com have been fabulous to work with for editing, project management, and all the things that I totally suck at.

Site Strategy

My new website(s) and approach are under development, and I'm happily working with Kevin McCarthy at www.360narrative.com. Websites can be cheap, but good ones don't have to be expensive, and the more important part is how it fits into the whole of your brand strategy.

Vendors

Over the years, the vendors of these technologies and related services have been my clients. Honorable mention, of course, goes to Citrix both for sponsoring this book and truly being a market leader. I'd like to acknowledge, however, the many that have been part of my journey: Accuconference, Adobe Connect, Brainshark, BlueStreak Learning, Business Expert Webinars, Conference Plus, The eLearning Experts, ePercipio, Everything Webinar, Joshua A. Jones, Ken Molay, Presentation Space, EventBuilder, EventSpan, InXpo, Integrated Marketing Partners, Intercall, Katie Stroud Learning Solutions, Maestro Conference, Microsoft Office Live Meeting/Lync, Pinnacle Performance, PGI, Quantum Leap Marketing, Talkpoint, Telenect, Virtual Venues, Webex, Webinar Base, Webinar Listings, Webcast to Learn, What Works Communications, and Yugma. And I've probably forgotten somebody, so apologies in advance.

ABOUT THE AUTHOR

Roger Courville is an internationally sought-after expert and analyst on the psychosocial aspects of "connectorship"—engaging people authentically with and through technology.

Once called "The Michael Jordan of virtual presentations," Roger is a multi-book author, award-winning writer, and multi-company entrepreneur. His work includes working with organizations as diverse as FedEx, American Express, US Bank, Australia Institute of Training and Development, and American Management Association.

By night, Roger volunteers on several nonprofit boards, as a taxi driver for his three kids, and as a guitar player for any band unlucky enough to have him.

Learn more at www.RogerCourville.com or by connecting here:

CV: thevirtualpresenter.com/curriculum-vitae/
Twitter: @RogerCourville
LinkedIn: linkedin.com/cc/rogerc
Facebook: facebook.com/valuesleuth

Better yet, pick up the phone. Really. +1.503.329.1662

Made in the USA
Middletown, DE
10 July 2015